A TASK UN

'An invaluable tool for all ministers
mittee.'

Stephen Gaukroger

'The world awaits a church with the whole world both in its heart and its focus . . . This book will help us become world Christians in world churches.'

Roger Forster

'This book gives a vision for those of us remaining in the UK in our home churches of what we can do and why we should do it. It contains a treasure trove of practical suggestions. I warmly recommend it.'

Viscountess Gill Brentford, OBE

'Practical and sanely revolutionary. If churches took this to heart, I would expect extraordinary blessing around the world.'

Dick Dowsett

'A vital and authoritative book – essential and challenging reading.'

Graham Mungeam,
Head of Overseas Department, Oasis Trust

'This book is much more strategic in these days than most people can imagine and I hope it will bring all of us into greater biblical action around the globe.'

George Verwer, Operation Mobilisation

'Michael Griffiths' new books stirs within us the excitement of seeing churches on fire for mission. This book will help churches understand, plan and prepare effectively for involvement in world mission.'

Malcolm McGregor,
Director of SIM UK/N. Europe

'The subject of this book is of vital importance for every local congregation . . . I warmly commend this book for individuals and for churches and pray that God will be able to speak powerfully through it.'

Richard Clark,
National Director, InterServe

'This book is long overdue. My hope is that through reading *A Task Unfinished*, today's church will not only embrace the vision for sending out workers overseas, but also discover the thrill of being in partnership with them as a supporting church.'

David Marfleet,
Deputy Chief Executive, MAF UK

'A contemporary book on mission from Mike Griffiths is welcome and packs a new challenge. I commend it to all who are serious in any way about Christ's great commission.'

David W Ellis,
National Director UK, OMF

'*A Task Unfinished* should be passed from friend to friend in each of our congregations. All in the Kingdom of God are needed. Each individual has a vital role to play if the "Unfinished Task" is to be "Finished".'

Michael Kelly,
British Director, World Horizons

'Mobilising the whole church for world mission – what a magnificent objective! And surely absolutely essential if we are to see a church for every people. But how can it be achieved? This book suggests a way.'

John T Bendor-Samuel,
Executive Director, Wycliffe Bible Translators

'Michael Griffiths always combines a sharp historical perspective, a wholehearted devotion to Scripture, a commitment to seeing the work of God move on through the church. He writes with the benefit of a lifetime spent advancing the cause of the gospel cross-culturally.'

Lindsay Brown, General Secretary, IFES

'The church, local, national and international seems to be becoming more central in the lives of Christians in the 1990s. We seem to be moving from a more individualistic approach to a greater corporate concern. I therefore positively recommend Michael's book as he helps us struggle with the issues involved in church and mission.'

John Chapman,
International Director, Latin Link

'In my opinion this book will prove to be an invaluable tool to the church for the task of world evangelism.'

Norman Barnes,
Director, Links International

'I'm thrilled that such a publication has been produced to tackle an area of church life that has been largely avoided, or neglected in recent years. In the past, almost by default, the church has devalued or abdicated its role of winning the world for Christ, by focusing only on the "goers". Without loyal, real, practical and informed "senders" the task-force is deficient. This is not a book for simply adding to a library, but a manual for effective daily service.'

Paul Lindsay,
Centre Director, Christian Service Centre

'This book fills a gap in our current resources. Michael's wealth of missionary experience, his wisdom and spiritual insight, and the pith and punch of his communication, make this a book to profit from and to enjoy.'

Robin Wells,
Africa Evangelical Fellowship (UK and Europe)

'A vital, indispensable book for every aspect of local church missionary strategy and care. It is disturbing and invigorating, and especially challenging to pastors. It is also a sheer relief to read such practical wisdom.'

Rev Geraint D Fielder,
author, broadcaster and conference speaker

'Michael Griffiths' books are always refreshing, dynamic and challenging. All new Christians need to hear the call to mission involvement. I hope they are gripped by their vital role in the "ninety-nine". Into Mission Mode is for all of us.'

Rt Rev David Evans,
General Secretary, South America Mission Society

'One of Michael Griffiths' God-given skills is the ability to arouse contemporary Christians to the challenges of mission, biblically understood. I hope the book will strengthen the conviction that to be a member of the church is also to be a member of God's missionary task-force, with no exceptions.'

Rev Timothy G Alford,
UK Director, Africa Inland Mission International

'Michael Griffiths at his best. Historical, biblical and contemporary – and all extremely readable.'

Michael Roemmele
FEBA Radio

'This book will be a vital source of guidance for many church leaders.'

Steve Bell
International Director, Action Partners

A Task Unfinished

How to recruit, support and pray for missionaries and Christian workers in a constantly changing world

MICHAEL GRIFFITHS

OMF International

MARC
Crowborough

British Library Cataloguing Data
A catalogue record for this book is available
from the British Library.

ISBN 1 85424 313 6

Designed and produced by Bookprint Creative Services
P.O. Box 827, BN21 3YJ, England for
MARC an imprint of Monarch Publications
Broadway House, The Broadway
Crowborough, East Sussex, TN6 1HQ.
Printed in Great Britain.

CONTENTS

INTRODUCTION

For almost forty years, I have been expected to speak on the need for congregations and individual Christians to obey the Great Commission. At the same time I have struggled for years, trying to discover how to teach congregations about world mission in a biblical way. Whenever I speak on the need for more labourers to serve in the international harvest field (and whether they are to be church-supported or self-financing is irrelevant at this stage), I wrestle with the problem of how to apply the call of Jesus or the challenge of Acts to every one of the rows of faces I see lifted towards me. I know perfectly well, and so do they, that only very few of my hearers are qualified or available to go out to other countries, as the church's missionary representatives. It just doesn't make sense to expect a congregation as a whole to respond to such a message. Along with other missionary speakers, almost in desperation, I have tried various solutions, for example:

1. Asking everyone to commit themselves to pray for missions.

2. Asking people to buy *Operation World* to keep on top of their TV sets.
3. Inviting them to ask the Chief Harvester to put each of them where he wants them to be, whether in this country or overseas.

But I remain unsatisfied: surely Scripture is relevant to every single believer, and not just to a few? I know that in preaching on singleness or on marriage, the other half of the congregation will feel left out, unless you take great care to include them. But when preaching on the need for missionaries, close to ninety-nine per cent may feel the message is not really relevant to them! So I feel uneasy, because I want to be relevant to everyone, and the bulk of even our most evangelical congregations seem unconvinced. They listen with commendable stoicism to a succession of missionary speakers, and may even give intellectual assent to what is said, but nothing changes very much. Is this the wrong target audience for this kind of sermon, more suitable for young people or college students perhaps? Or is it that my approach has been in some way distorted and eccentric, and not totally biblical in its emphasis? When Paul writes his letters he seems to assume that the believers to whom he writes are all involved in his ministry and eager and willing to pray for him.

False Distinctions

I believe the New Testament shows us greater freedom and flexibility in fulfilling Christ's mandate to make disciples of all nations than we allow ourselves. We have become somewhat fossilized and we create our own traditional straitjackets. We have created distinctions between lay people and ministers, or full time and part time, or missionaries and 'tent makers'.[1] I doubt whether New Testament people thought that way at all: Christians were just Christians, with a common commitment to the cause of Christ. I plead therefore for a return to biblical versatility, where there seem to have been no rigid distinctions between clergy and laity, nor between ministers and missionaries, nor between self-supporting and church-supported workers. The disciples of Jesus were all disciples, and all were expected to be equally committed to their Teacher's cause, and equally concerned to take the gospel to the ends of the earth.

'The whole church must take the whole gospel to the whole world' is a fine slogan, but how can we make it happen? It is theologically correct, and intellectually satisfying, but how does one persuade whole congregations to embrace it? Everybody is so busy with their packed daily lives: how in reality can every believer make mission part of their daily Christian experience? Is there, realistically, a credible role in world mission we can offer to the ninety-nine per cent of Christians who remain 'at home'?

I believe there is. And I believe this is the single most important issue in world mission. Several years ago I wrote a small booklet for OMF, called *Get your Church involved in Missions*. It was widely used, and even translated into other languages. Later, owing to the illness of Harry Sutton, I was invited to step in to edit a book called *Ten Sending Churches*.[2] Since then the development of the Association of Church Mission Committees in the United States and Canada has encouraged an increasing literature, notably its own excellent Handbook.[3] In North America there have been books by Paul Borthwick[4] and more recently an excellent book by Neal Pirolo.[5] In Britain *Love your Local Missionary*[6] also covered this important area. So why do we need another?

Some Real Progress

I was sitting in on our own local church mission committee in Guildford recently, and was impressed by the commitment of the members, and the good questions they were asking a returning missionary. We can be glad that there has been significant progress in British churches too. Many local churches now have their own mission committees, with policies on selection, screening, training, sending and support which are known to all the membership. We may not have noticed it, but there has been a real advance and development in this area today as compared with the fifties. It is now widely recognised that realistic 'support' must be directed toward helping the whole person, and not merely supplying money. Fresh recognition of the reality of 'spiritual warfare' (not as a trendy factional obsession, but something which has always been understood among evangelical missionaries) has deepened the perception that prayer for mission work is far, far more than mentioning the missionaries by name once a week during a minister's pastoral prayer, and indeed involves 'labouring'[7] in prayer. But it is still uncommon to find a congregation totally mobilised for world mission, in the extraordinary way that the church at Herrnhut was (see pp. 53, 122–3).

Neal Pirolo[8] makes the helpful analogy between the nine soldiers in support roles for every one in the front line, and points out that 'sending', when properly understood, is every bit as much missionary service as 'going'. Compared with the relatively small proportion of those actually sent to engage in cross-cultural mission, there is a much larger team of supporters standing behind them, and sending them. When this is properly understood and implemented, it really does provide a role relating to all nations for all Christians, including the vast majority who stay at home in their own country and culture. Sending is just as much part of obedience as going, and caring about and praying about sending is a role for every 'normal' Christian.

Why Another Book?

My former beloved mission, OMF International (formerly the China Inland Mission), and Tony Collins of Monarch, have been urging me to try to write something more detailed on this subject. I did question whether we really need another book, but recognise that the world scene and the church scene in which we live is constantly changing. We all have a remarkable knack for picking up new jargon without making real and lasting changes to deal with our underlying sloth and apathy. Taking on the outward words and forms of contemporary godliness is always easier than making genuine behavioural changes. In language learning, we can always recognise and comprehend words and phrases, long before we actually use them when we talk ourselves. In a similar way, spiritually we often merely give verbal assent to good ideas and ideal behaviour patterns. This is not because we need to discover some fresh secret or new methodology, but because we fail to implement old truths that we know in our heads, but have never done anything about.

My prayer is that this book may help some of us to take some fresh steps forward. We need to move on from mere polite acquiescence to mission goals, to accepting the need of all round 'support' for human beings sent into cross cultural situations, to deepening involvement and genuine bonding with them in what is not just 'their work', but 'our work', as Christ's church. This parallels what Marxists used to call 'politicisation of the masses'. We want to persuade all Christian believers that they can become truly involved in world mission. Failure to do this effectively has been the chief reason for church decline in Europe.

THE MAIN THESIS OF THIS BOOK

Every local church shares in the call to make disciples of all nations, and must mobilise its activities to that end. The local body of Christ is committed to pro-active spiritual 'staff development' for all its members. The local church is the nursery of missions. For every individual member chosen to go out to the cross cultural 'front-line' there need to be ninety-nine committed supporters standing behind them. This means that if we want to implement 'every member ministry', that must include a significant, active role in missions for every church member, quite apart from those who themselves go overseas.

Notes

1 Self-supporting workers overseas, taken from Paul's profession as a tent maker.
2 Ed. Michael Griffiths, *Ten Sending Churches*, (London: MARC Europe; STL; Evangelical Missionary Alliance, 1985).
3 *Church Missions Policy Handbook*, (Wheaton, Ill.: Association of Church Missions Committees, 1987).
4 Paul Borthwick, *A Mind for Missions*, (Colorado: Navpress 1987); *Youth and Missions*, (Wheaton, Ill.: Scripture Press, 1988); *How to be a World Class Christian*, (Wheaton, Ill.: Scripture Press, 1991).
5 Neal Pirolo, *Serving as Senders*, (OM Publishing 1996).
6 Ed. Martin Goldsmith, *Love your Local Missionary*, (London: MARC Europe, STL, Evangelical Missionary Alliance, 1984).
7 Philippians 4:12, 13.
8 Neal Pirolo, *Serving as Senders*.

CHAPTER I

THE CHANGING DIMENSIONS OF WORLD MISSION

1. The Changing World

There are more countries open to the Gospel than at any time since the 1914–18 War, and far more people living in them than ever before.

In 1950 I heard a little old lady wearing strings of beads speak to a group of us students over breakfast. Outward appearances are deceptive. Mildred Cable looked as though she had never been out of Kensington. I learned later that she had been headmistress of a girls' school in China, until at the age of forty-five she answered God's call to travel out along the Silk Road from north-west China preaching Christ, and she and two other women in their fifties journeyed in ox carts across the Gobi desert into Xinjiang. At our meeting she opened her handbag, and used a small pocket Testament to show us how the doors of walled cities in the Gobi Desert slowly close at dusk. That, she said, is what is happening now in China: the door is closing. That was the year that Communist China closed its doors to foreign missionaries, though Russian advance had closed Xinjiang some years earlier.

In my student days the Iron Curtain had already shut us off from the Soviet Union and Eastern Europe, and now China was closed off as well. No wonder all my generation grew up talking of 'closed countries'. We accepted that political forces were closing off large sections of the globe to missionary endeavour. Only later did people like Brother Andrew and George Verwer demonstrate that there was no such thing as a closed country. New items like 'limited access' and 'creative access' entered our vocabulary and it became a challenge to Christian ingenuity to find ways of crossing frontiers, bearing God's good news, even if people put barriers in the way. If the doors were closed, there were always windows of opportunity!

There were always some doors opening as well as others closing. Nepal opened for the first time in 1953, while I was still in theological college. Later refugees from Tibet and Afghanistan made it possible to reach peoples who had been virtually inaccessible for many years. At the same time, those urging the importance of so-called 'tent making' were arguing that more and more countries were closing and that by the end of the century ninety per cent of countries needing to be evangelised would be closed to 'conventional missionaries'.

To some extent all that has changed, and in these last five years we have seen more countries open to the messengers of the gospel (however described in their passports) than at any time in the present century. Recently at Beersheba in Israel I was talking to 'Russians' of Jewish descent, who had found Christ in Uzbekistan and Tajikistan.

'Church-supported' missionaries are a development of the past two hundred years; before then everyone had been 'self-supporting' since the days of Acts. Realising this fact has brought a much greater flexibility to the whole concept of 'being a missionary'. Only yesterday I had a letter from someone going into a 'creative access' country asking their

'Supporters Club' (they actually call it that) to stop using the 'M-words' about them, as they will be in secular business: the word 'missionary' would hinder their ministry for Christ in the somewhat hostile climate they would be entering.

All this underlines the fact that while such countries even now may not be open to 'conventional missionaries', they are open to Christians who can find an appropriate way of getting in, and staying in (see Chapter VIII).

Not only are more countries open to the Gospel, but there is also an increasing ethnic and pluralistic mix of populations.

The increasing mobility of human populations and the number of political and economic refugees means that huge Islamic, Hindu and Chinese 'Buddhist' communities have been established in countries that used to be regarded as Christian. There are now three million Muslims living in the UK.

This is sometimes stated as 'the mission field coming to us, instead of us needing to go to the mission field'. However modern attitudes to pluralism, and the view that changing another's belief is somehow racist and intolerant, has meant that not many churches have been effective in evangelism among Muslims and Hindus. There have also, of course, been practical difficulties in crossing language and culture barriers, especially with the older generation.

I retain a vivid impression of sitting outside a fine evangelical church, watching a stream of men in turbans and women in saris walk past to and from their homes in the street, to find when the service began only one Asian person inside the church building, and he a Chinese. There may be more successful evangelism when our Christian teenagers are able to witness to their peers among second generation Asian young people whose language and cultural understanding are closer to ours.

There is also sadly the opposite phenomenon of 'ethnic cleansing' and partition of populations along ethnic lines, especially where those ethnic groups have particular religious affinities – with Roman Catholicism, Orthodoxy or Islam, as in the former Yugoslavia.

2. The Changing Shape of 'Missionaries'

In our third year teaching in Vancouver, we occupied the apartment of a recently married young couple, who spent the year teaching English in Ulan Bator in Mongolia. The husband later returned there for one month to give some help to a company which was paying his return airfare and expenses: the firm that employed him specialised in making tents out of goat skins, just as Aquila and Priscilla's firm had employed the apostle Paul as a 'tent maker' nineteen hundred years ago! Being a native English speaker and having the skill to teach is proving a remarkably useful 'passport' into a wide range of countries.

Recently my wife and I visited a secular state in the Middle East and were fascinated to discover the variety of routes that the Lord had used to bring Christian men and women to work and witness in that country. There are a number of different categories:

A. Long term church-supported

We met an American Mennonite couple working in a Christian hospital that has served an Arabic speaking community for many, many years. We met a Christian Jordani representing the Bible Society in the area. And we met just one conventional missionary church planter, working with Arabic speaking churches. I have put this group first, as the one we would think of as fulfilling the traditional missionary calling, but it was probably the smallest, albeit significant, category of workers.

B. Long term self-supporting

Andy is a university lecturer, graduate of a prestigious American university, who first enrolled there as a student. After a year he was invited to teach on the faculty. He has now held resident status for fourteen years and been active in work among international students.

Bill grew up abroad, but studied theology in Scotland. He enrolled for post-graduate studies in a university, and supported himself by helping to run an ambulance service at night. He had a tourist visa to start with, but volunteered to join the army for which he required resident status – and got it! After that he was able to apply for citizenship and was granted that as well. This is 'creative access' indeed! But you can see that it demands a total sacrificial willingness to identify with your new country. You must show that you want to belong, and to do something useful for the land of your adoption.

Chris first arrived with a short-term mission team. His testimony was that he had no sooner landed than he felt 'this is where the Lord wants me to be'. But he had a much more difficult time winning acceptance, faced expulsion and went through six years of court cases before he was able to gain permanent residence. For him identification has meant several years of military service, including active service in a war, and getting shot up by one of their own planes. He supports his family by working for a company. He and his wife are active in a local Christian congregation. This example shows the determination needed to stick fast, when humanly speaking it looks impossible to stay, as well as demonstrating the lengths to which he was willing to go to prove his commitment to his adopted nation.

C. Grown children of long term residents

This is an interesting group of individuals born to parents working overseas, who love their adopted countries and have decided to stay there for life. MKs ('missionary kids') have their own special identity problems, and most of our thinking in the past has tried to give them education that enables them to identify with their parents' home countries. Neither in Asia, nor in Africa generally, is it possible for Caucasian children to totally identify (because of their washed out appearance and big noses), but both in Europe and Latin America it is possible for such children to speak the language perfectly and to become themselves Europeans or Latin Americans. I recall a Frenchman interpreting for me in Paris, who had a Scottish grandfather who went as a missionary to Brittany!

Few of us would want to commit our children to continue in the countries where we have been serving, for it cannot be assumed that they will all necessarily become Christians even: they are free agents. However in this country we met two second generation men, continuing to live and work in the country their parents had felt God had called them to work in. And while we cannot plan for this, the Chief Harvester in his sovereignty can certainly ordain it.

Dave was one of Chris's children, and though speaking English with an American accent, felt more fluent in the national language than in English. He has done three years of military service, and attends Christian meetings in the national language. He is currently on a short-term evangelism project in North America.

Ed's parents worked at a Christian hospital, and he grew up speaking three languages fluently. He has a doctorate in Archaeology, and is one of Britain's few active field archaeologists, involved in several significant excavations within the country. He is a founder member of the national evangelical student movement.

D. International students

'Overseas students' go right back to the Book of Daniel.[1] We met several international students in the capital city, many of whom had come to study the national language. They were of assorted nationalities – American, British, Canadian, Chinese, Dutch, Japanese, Korean, and Swedish. I have known a number who have deliberately enrolled for advanced degrees in restricted access countries in order to witness for Christ. Long before the Berlin Wall came down, many African students from Ghana and Nigeria ran Bible studies for students in Moscow and Kiev. One problem is that intellectually brilliant students who win scholarships to study abroad tend to be academic types, not necessarily gifted in evangelism. The late Colin Hemer, New Testament scholar, author of a very up-market book on Acts,[2] and an expert on the Seven Churches of Asia Minor, and biblical sites in Turkey generally, was an exception. He spoke Turkish, and his home was always open to Turkish students.

This university channel is a route for self-supporting Christian workers that needs to be considered seriously by those who have the academic credentials and abilities that make it possible. There are prestigious universities in various fields in different countries where the Christian research student may be an effective witness.

E. Short-term visitors

We bumped into an old school friend of mine, recently retired from being a schoolmaster, and his wife who were giving several weeks to helping in a Christian outreach to tourists. We also met a retired American couple, who had been in mission administration at home. After retirement they came out and gave a whole year to studying the national language. They offer to 'house sit' for various missionary and academic friends while they are on home leave, and the husband does some preaching in local churches. In these days of early retirement, there are a whole group of people in our churches, in their late fifties and early sixties, who could be self-supporting financially, but who need the prayer support of their sending churches.

We ourselves were there for the annual national student conference as part-time workers with IFES, the International Fellowship of Evangelical Students.

This brief survey from just one country demonstrates how missionary patterns are changing, achieving greater flexibility, and finding a variety of different ways of living in a country. It may all seem very unstructured and untidy to some, but we need to see that the chief missioner himself, our missionary Lord, is really mustering his raggletaggle troops, aiding them through His Holy Spirit. So it is organised by the 'Chief Harvester'[3] and not by us, and all the better for it. The onus is on us, however, to work together in a way that produces co-operation, and not competition.

For those of us with tidy minds who like to see everything neat and orderly, this variety of possible routes may seem very messy and unsatisfactory. If this were entirely a matter of human organisation, that might well be the case, but if we believe that the 'Chief Harvester' is overseeing and guiding his labourers to bring in his harvest, then we shall not worry. The Lord rarely if ever seems to do the same thing twice, and each individual has their own special pilgrimage. I am not denying that there may be some unsanctified individualism going on that may not be pleasing to him, but I am insisting that, in his sovereignty, he delights as much in his motley collection of irregulars, as in the more disciplined ranks of more conventional mission bodies.

F. Two of the unconventionals

There always have been some very unusual and irregular Christians attached to the missionary body. Consider John

Athelstan Cheese (there really was such a person) who had so little money, that he once tried to travel by ship as a piece of luggage. Asked what he lived on, he replied : 'Oh rice, and dates, . . . and did I say, rice?' A Somali once commented of him, that it was a pity he was not a Muslim, but that he was undoubtedly the most holy man in Somaliland! Or Joseph Wolff (1795–1862), son of a Jewish rabbi, educated as a Catholic, who studied in the Collegio di Propaganda Fide in Rome, and was expelled for questioning papal infallibility. Escaping to England, he studied with Charles Simeon at Cambridge, and became one of the first missionaries of the London Society for the Propagation of Christianity among the Jews (today called the Church's Ministry among Jewish People). He was naturalised as British and married Lady Georgiana Walpole, granddaughter of Prime Minister Sir Robert Walpole. He was accomplished in fourteen languages, preached in nine, but could not shave himself, cook for himself, swim or ride a horse. He was once sold into slavery and three times condemned to death. All very untidy, and eccentric, but the hand of the Lord was on him during his extraordinary travels. The Lord seems to rejoice in these eccentric irregulars, who fit our usual categories uneasily, and yet can be so fruitful for him. The current situation offers more options than it ever has before. There is plenty of room for flexible irregulars!

However it is the trend to more self-supporting workers, discussed in Chapter VIII, which I believe is the most significant. Many countries, reluctant to accept 'missionaries' are none the less open to receive people, whom they know to be Christians,[4] working in medicine, teaching, engineering, business and so on. This will have to be the wave of the future, if the '10–40 window'[5] countries are to have a Christian presence, and a growing number of indigenous Christian churches.

It is also true of China. Whereas all foreigners had to leave in 1949, when Mao came to power, the government is actively recruiting some three to five thousand foreign people every year now, to help its modernisation.

3. The Changing Patterns of General Support

There continue to be marked changes in church life:

i. *Increasing geographical mobility*: this means an increasingly rapid turnover of congregations, so that half of the church members may have left, and the other half of church members be new when a missionary returns to his home church after a four or five year absence overseas. This makes it harder for church members to feel that they really know the missionaries that the church (as it was a few years earlier) has sent out.

ii. *Changes in wealth distribution*: in the early years of interdenominational missions a few very rich donors could send personal cheques. Notice the one generous donor supporting five missionaries singlehanded in the Broomhall quote below (p. 29). Today there are fewer people with large private incomes, but a much larger middle income group, some of whom are not yet organised in budgeting for regular giving, and maximising it through covenants and the like.

iii. *Increasing mobility of young people*: more and more leave home for some kind of tertiary education, as much as a third of the population. Britain had twenty universities in 1954 and a hundred and six in 1994: a fivefold expansion in forty years. This means that people who have grown up in a single 'home church' are now rare. Many Christian young people converted in their teens will have experienced in addition to their original 'home' congregation, a church in a university city (which they may or may not have actually joined), perhaps a church in another place for postgraduate or professional training, and yet other churches in places of their first employment. This means that often people have 'grown away' from their home church, but not been long enough in any other single congregation to be regarded as 'really one of ours'. This situation can be especially acute for medics and nurses. There is a huge problem for popular churches which attract a lot of students, or, worse still, a lot of theological and Bible College students. So here are keen committed Christians, who are unclear about where their church loyalties lie, and therefore will find it difficult to become church supported missionaries.

But there are compensations. Whereas in the past people might once have known few Christians outside their own congregation, today's twenty-something Christian considering serving the Lord overseas has a whole range of Christian friends from school, college or university, employment, Christian camps and missions, and Bible training colleges, some of whom may well be eager to help with prayer and financial support.

iv. *Changes in church life.* Whereas at the start of the century, the vast majority of Christians were (alphabetically) Anglicans, Baptists, Brethren, Congregationalists, Methodists or Presbyterians, today there is a much wider and more varied spectrum. This has been the consequence of the Charismatic movement, and the resulting church divisions. Many who grew up in Brethren assemblies, and were dissatisfied with them, started independent house churches. Some of us may welcome change, and the church revolution which has taken place, even if others deplore it: either way you cannot ignore history.

The proliferation of church groupings has led also to a proliferation of sending agencies. Some newer churches may wish to create their own sending agencies rather than use the older ones. They may learn from the mistakes of older agencies, or through ignorance repeat them. The churches should learn from past experience, but do not always do so. The effect of proliferation is certainly to widen the options, but it makes decisions about which sending agency to choose more complex both for churches and for individuals.

v. *The Charismatic movement*: this is often said to have widened people's understanding of the Person and Work of the Holy Spirit, and in some circles this is certainly true. However through the Keswick Convention movement, and in missions generally, there always has been a strong consciousness among missionaries of their need for empowering by the Holy Spirit, as well as his work in opening the eyes of blinded hearers. Long before the Charismatic movement began, the need for spiritual gifts was widely taught, and we prayed for the exercise of these gifts in missionary ministry. Revivals in Korea, China, and East Africa all deepened missionary awareness of the Spirit's work. While there has been a wider perception of the work of the Holy Spirit, (and some hype), the statistics (with some glorious exceptions) do not seem to show increased effectiveness in evangelism, or more long term missionaries sent out. The heightened awareness of spiritual warfare is dealt with later in Chapter VII, though it does not always seem to have resulted in more prayer for the spread of the Gospel.

4. The Changing Patterns of Financial Support

We are so used to present day patterns we forget that prior to 1800 almost all missionaries had to finance themselves. There was no way Matteo Ricci (1552–1610), a Jesuit living in Peking, could have been supported from his native Italy. He supported himself by clock making and repairing, and making maps. The Moravians supported themselves as carpenters or traders. William Carey (1761–1834) first supported himself as manager of an indigo plantation and later by teaching as a professor in Calcutta. Only with the development of international banks did things begin to change, though transferring money overseas was a lengthy and uncertain process. Hudson Taylor (1832–1905) in early years would visit the agents in Canton hoping that a bank draft had arrived for him, that he could cash with the Hong Kong and Shanghai Bank.

However it is easy to assume that from that time onwards, almost all missionaries became church-supported. This was not actually the case, as I realised recently when I came across the following address given just over one hundred years ago by Benjamin Broomhall to the Annual Meeting of CIM supporters. This shows that even within missionary societies the move to being church supported was only partial, and not as hard and fast a change as I had first thought:

. . . of the 390 missionaries now in China, who have gone from England (there were 66 others from North America and Australia, and 118 Associates from other European countries), there are thirty two labouring at their own expense; there are eighty seven supported entirely by friends, and sixteen partly supported, leaving 255 to be provided entirely from the mission funds. One friend supports five missionaries; three friends support two each; and thirty nine friends support one each. In two cases two friends support one between them; so that fifty-two are thus kindly provided for. There are thirty five others who are supported by Associations; or Sunday Schools or particular churches. That is a thing for which we are specially thankful. I hope that the day will come in connection with all missionary organisations when churches and associations, and even families, will charge themselves with the entire cost of a missionary.[6]

Today we need to show the same degree of flexibility in matters of financial support. However, recent years have shown that financial support is far less important than spiritual and moral support: and that even when there is no need for financial support eg of a totally self-financing 'tentmaker', there remains a continuing need for prayer support and morale boosting encouragement.

Then, of course, there are 'home missions' which need financial and prayer support in the same way. There are thus at least four categories of 'mission' to be considered for support from any local church budget:

1. Same country, same culture. (eg UCCF staff, Scripture Union etc.).
2. Same country, different culture (eg reaching Asians in Britain).
3. Overseas country, same culture (eg reaching expatriates abroad)
4. Overseas country, different culture (ie cross-cultural mission).

For home mission and for overseas missions, there are those 'on the frontline' and others giving back-up. That back-up is wide-ranging. There are those who are responsible for strategy, for pastoral care of workers, for recruiting and training new candidates, for reflecting news back to the Christian public, for all the needed administration, and so forth. We shouldn't overlook these needs, and can be in danger of doing so as there has been a significant shift away from supporting 'societies' (whether working at home or overseas) to supporting individuals working for them in 'front line' roles. It is always noticeably harder for home staff of missionary societies to generate support than it is for their fellows who are working overseas. We must not underestimate the role that these people play.

Notes

1 Daniel. 1:4, 5, 17—the first of three Babylonian deportations of Israelis. Verse 3 indicates that these were chosen as especially gifted individuals.

2 Colin J. Hemer, *The Book of Acts in the Setting of Hellenistic History*, (Tubingen: Mohr, 1989).

3 Matthew 9:38; Luke 10:2.

4 We are naive if we believe, for example, that Chinese intelligence services are unaware that it is Christian faith that has motivated numbers of western people to work in China. They would rather have Christians than people who would bring drugs or AIDS into China, just so long as nobody is too blatant or confrontational about it. There are polite courtesies, well recognised in Asian tactful face saving.

5 The band of countries between 10° and 40° latitude N, which are largely Muslim.

6 Benjamin Broomhall, *China's Millions*, 1894.

CHAPTER II

THE KEY ROLE OF THE LOCAL CHURCH

As we perceive in the Bible, the local church is the real nursery for developing Jesus' witnesses for transplantation. It was in the local church where the first witnesses, after the apostles, were equipped with wisdom and power to shake the world, and it is witnesses raised under the Spirit's guidance from this same origin, who are needed to do that today. It is extremely important that the church does everything in its power to raise these up.'[1]

Fredrik Franson

I like this picture of the local church as a nursery or seed-bed for growing missionaries. If you travel in eastern Asia in the spring, you will see that only a few small plots of ground have been sown with seed and are now green with closely packed rice seedlings. The much wider area of surrounding paddy fields still lie bare and empty. When the seedlings have grown, the main fields are flooded and lines of workers may be seen knee deep in the mud, planting out the seedlings from the small nursery beds in neat well-spaced lines in all the surrounding fields. So how do we interpret this allegorical picture? The local church is the seedling bed, close packed with Christians. The seedlings are individual Christians who have been nurtured and matured in the local church. The surrounding fields are the wider world around us. The Christian workers who have grown in the local church then need to be planted out, and spaced out around the world as part of a great harvest.

Mission is not the concern of just a few enthusiasts, but of the whole church: we need to send our best qualified members to places where they can be most useful. But this must be a cooperative, corporate enterprise in which every single church member is able to feel involved. Ants and social wasps and bees function in colonies, where some remain to work in the hive or nest, while others are sent out to forage and harvest in the world around: they seem to have got their act together very well and certainly better than us.[2]

> Each local church has an evangelistic mission in the world, and for this mission the church needs to mobilise itself, including all of its individual members.
>
> Fredrik Franson[3]

Contrasting with Franson's two very positive statements about the role of the local church, is the sad comment of Hendrik Kraemer, written in 1938:

> The missionary cause is the cause of a decided minority in the churches, and only a part even of this minority shoulders its share in the missionary task with the real intelligence of real faith.[4]

This challenge to us regarding 'the real intelligence of real faith' is one we must face up to. In much of our talk about mission, we seem to assume there is some mysterious pool of manpower somewhere else from which missionaries may be provided. There is no such pool. If we obey Christ's command to pray for labourers, then they must all come from local churches, including ours. There is no other source. If the Gospel is to be taken to the ends of the earth, preached to all nations, and the huge unevangelised blocs of Muslims, Hindus and Buddhists are to have the opportunity of responding to Christ, then it is our local churches which must send out some of our own members to fulfil Christ's command. There is no other source outside the local churches where manpower and womanpower may be found to fulfil our God-given task.

In much common thinking, we are taught that churches exist for worship, for teaching, for fellowship, for evangelism and social service. World mission is usually seen as an extra, a supplement for enthusiasts. Rarely do we find churches who appreciate that mission is just as much a responsibility of the local church, as worship is. The last words of Jesus to the eleven are not 'Go and form a worshipping community' but 'Go and make disciples of all nations, baptising them and teaching them to obey everything I have commanded you'. It is a mission commission, not a worship commission. To express it this way may prove unpopular in some circles, but we need to rethink some of our commonly-held assumptions by returning to Scripture. An impartial observer would have to say that in the Acts and the Epistles mission is emphasized and worship is not. We have become quite eccentric and lopsided in our emphases!

The danger of being a local church – and the very use of the expression encourages this – is that we limit ourselves to parish or town or neighbourhood and only think of our local responsibilities. The command to go and make disciples, and to teach everyone to obey all that Jesus taught, including going to make disciples, cannot be delegated to some external body. There is no such body. There are only local churches, and they have the responsibility to send some of their members beyond their own local environs, and national environment, into all the world to preach the Gospel.

There are things that local churches cannot do well, because we do not have sufficient resources within a single congregation. To achieve some of our biblical goals, we may have to cooperate together with other local churches: to print Bibles, treat leprosy, broadcast the Gospel, treat drug addicts, help AIDS patients, provide Christian materials for the blind and so on. Thus voluntary societies drawing Christians from many local churches specialise in tackling tasks that no single local church could ever hope to achieve. Missionary societies perform similar functions in relation to geographical areas, or specialised ministries. But while we may delegate responsibility to specialist groups, the men and women who engage in such ministries all have to come from local churches. There is no other reserve of manpower to draw upon. Societies must not usurp responsibilities that belong to local churches, and local churches must not abdicate responsibilities that are properly theirs. Certainly, there are some things that missionary societies can do, which for geographical reasons local churches cannot do: but correspondingly there are things that local churches can and must do, that lie beyond the abilities of societies. The role of Bible and missionary training colleges is also part of the mix, and I have listed the three areas of complementary ministries for thought and consideration. Few lists are exhaustive, but they do give some idea of how all of us in God's universal church need one another and need to cooperate creatively.

What the Local Church Can and Should Do Better Than Any Society

1. Develop initial discipleship training within the church family.

2. Provide opportunities for developing spiritual gifts.
3. Give an objective assessment of long term potential.
4. Give more training to selected individuals.
5. Recommend people to missionary training colleges.
6. Provide financial support during college missionary training.
7. Assist in the practical arrangements for departure.
8. Commission missionaries by laying on hands.
9. Provide realistic financial support according to actual needs.
10. Continue communication of loving concern, and moral support.
11. Care for the parents of the missionary left behind.
12. Give pastoral care and feed 'drained empties' on home leave.
13. Provide a role in the local church and continued 'in-training'.
14. Care for the children of missionaries.
15. Ensure that the needs of retired missionaries are met.

What Missionary Societies Do Better Than Local Churches.

1. Have detailed knowledge and experience of living and working in specific overseas situations.
2. Know or provide the best language schools.
3. Provide opportunities for bonding with national believers.
4. Provide ongoing orientation to culture, society and religions.
5. Provide informed medical service, advice on innoculations, preventative medicine etc.
6. Provide immediate pastoral care during the difficult time of induction.

7. Give experienced oversight of the new missionary's work and relationships.
8. Provide support services – obtaining visas, forwarding baggage, transferring money, arranging inoculations, police permits etc.
9. Provide immediate communication in emergencies, and regular news of the work and of the missionary.
10. Provide a prayerful support structure in the overseas situation.
11. Link the worker with other Christian organisations in the area or country.
12. Determine policies and strategies on basis of local experience.
13. Act as a middleman between missionaries and receiving churches.
14. Provide and supervise children's schooling.
15. Assess the missionary's progress in language and ministry, and report back on it to the sending churches.

What Bible and Missionary Training Colleges Can Do That Most Local Churches Cannot

1. Provide a whole group of gifted teachers qualified across a wide range of biblical, theological and practical disciplines.
2. Provide daily oversight and pastoral care of those studying with them.
3. Provide peer group fellowship with highly motivated and committed friends.
4. Provide cross cultural training by experienced workers.
5. As a result of sustained daily contact, provide assess-

ment of individuals' strengths, weaknesses and suitability for service.

6. Help a person develop in an all-round way and not just in cognitive knowledge and ministry skills.

7. Provide library facilities on a scale not possible for local church.

8. Provide recognised qualifications in an accredited programme.

9. Provide the opportunity for sustained close fellowship with those of other races, nationalities and backgrounds in everyday situations.

10. Provide the opportunity for Christians to meet those from other churches and benefit from other evangelical traditions.

What Churches Can Do For Their Members That Nobody Else Can

1. Morale support

No, not a misprint for 'moral', for giving somebody 'moral support' may mean you assure them you are with them, but do little about it! The word 'support' suggests to most people that we are talking about money. But support needs to be something much more holistic than just sending money to support a missionary. 'Support' means giving practical and verbal expression to friendship and encouragement. When David was fleeing from Saul in the wilderness of Ziph, Jonathan sought him out and 'strengthened his hand in God' (1 Samuel 23:16). We all need 'Jonathans', male and female, to come alongside and encourage us. When Paul was in prison in Rome, a man called Onesiphorus took pains to keep on visiting him: 'he often refreshed me' (2 Timothy 1:16). People need to know that they have friends and supporters who love them and are concerned about them. It is this kind of support for morale which is so crucial.

There are the opposite kind of people too, unfortunately, like those who gathered around Job, and though well meaning, discouraged him. Or like those who deliberately sought to discourage and distract Nehemiah (Nehemiah 6:9,10). At the time when Vietnam fell to the Vietcong, Lao to the Pathet Lao and Cambodia to the Khmer Rouge all within a few days, well meaning people influenced by the domino theory were writing to missionary friends in Thailand asking: 'Have you got your stuff packed? Are you ready to go?' My own father, wanting to see more of us, said to me after a few years: 'Don't you think you have done your bit now?' Love and concern may not always be concerned to seek first God's kingdom and his righteousness. The classic discouragement story comes from John Paton, where a 'dear old Christian gentleman' kept on saying:

'The cannibals. You will be eaten by cannibals!' Paton replied:

'Mr Dickson, you are advanced in years now, and your own prospect is soon to be laid in the grave, there to be eaten by worms; I confess to you that if I can but live and die serving and honouring the Lord Jesus, it will make no difference to me whether I am eaten by cannibals or by worms.'[5]

Support and encouragement come in many forms. Letters are always welcome. These days telephone calls are relatively cheap, and they can provide a more immediate sense of belonging and being cared for, and a growing number of missionaries are now on E-mail.

Church members may be travelling on business, and can fit in time for a visit. A tour by pastors or elders visiting several missionaries on one trip can be a great blessing if the church can afford it. We were with Jim and Ann Graham of

Gold Hill Baptist Church speaking at the Hong Kong Keswick recently, and for them the highlight was the opportunity to visit members of their own church working out in the New Territories.

Morale is a funny thing: it takes relatively small things sometimes to depress people and make them feel miserable. By the same token it takes relatively small things to warm their hearts and encourage them. Just a few well chosen words in a letter or on a card can make all the difference, like the sun suddenly appearing through the clouds.

2A. *Practical support at the time of first departure*

This is a brief time of intense effort. It can be very exhausting for those who are being sent out, and they will need a lot of help in preparing to move themselves and their belongings to a distant place. It needs imaginative caring to know how to help best.

(i). *Packing baggage*. Sometimes sending books through the post at the maximum weight for parcels is cheaper than sending them sea freight. The whole business of roping and labelling trunks and boxes is time-consuming and helping people to carry heavy baggage downstairs, especially if they are older, is much appreciated.

(ii). *Storage space*. If people have no permanent house of their own, they will need somewhere to store the goods they are leaving behind. It may be that the church has some under-utilised storage space, or someone in the church with a bigger house may offer to store such things for those leaving. That needs some strong younger people to help carry the stuff to where it needs to be stored.

(iii). *Selling a vehicle*. There will probably be a car to be sold; they may well hope to get it advertised and sold before they leave, but what if it does not sell? And maybe they need to keep on using it until near to the day of departure.

Somebody can help by offering to arrange for the car to be sold after the missionaries have left.

2B. *Practical support while missionaries are abroad.*

This requires a sustained, long-term commitment to keep on helping in a whole variety of practical ways.

(i). *Managing a rented house.* If the departing missionary owns their own house, and wants to keep it for when they return, and can keep up mortgage payments by taking in tenants, then they need someone to keep an eye on the house, ensure that rents are being paid on time, that the rental agreement is being observed, and if the first tenants leave, to find new tenants. This can be a time-consuming job, but one impossible for missionaries to do themselves when they live thousands of miles away.

(ii). *Handling financial matters.* There may well be tax returns to complete each year, or borough taxes to be paid. Nowadays banks can arrange to handle a great deal by direct debit and so on, but there is nearly always a need for someone to be available to handle any problem that might arise unexpectedly. There will be magazine subscriptions and other memberships that have to be paid and renewed.

(iii). *Sending out a prayer letter.* This always needs organising: getting prayer letters printed, as nicely but as cheaply as possible, and getting envelopes addressed, stuffed, stamped and posted is a humdrum and time-consuming ministry, but if it helps more people to get involved in the work by praying for it, it is well worthwhile. Even keeping the address list, or data base, up to date with changing addresses in our highly mobile society is a great help. Good layout may not be a gift of the missionary, but it may be the gift of someone else. There may even be a need for a little editing!

(iv). *Keeping them in touch.* There are a number of different ways, especially if a little imagination is used.

Books. The more literary-inclined missionary will really appreciate copies of significant books both secular and spiritual as they come out. In our early language-learning years, we suddenly realised that we were hungry for books in English. In a shop in a major Japanese city we found collections of English, Russian and Welsh short stories, and we still treasure all three. Has there been a book (or video) of an appreciated BBC series recently?

Magazines. My father took out a subscription to *Good Housekeeping* for my wife and renewed it faithfully each year. Many of us took out subscriptions to *The Times Weekly* when it existed, and then *The Guardian Weekly*. There were always copies of *Readers Digest*, *Time* and *Newsweek* around, but we wanted more news from our own home country, and helpful political comment, so that we knew how people were thinking. Again *Christianity Today* was sometimes available, but we needed more news of British churches, activities and individuals. *Evangelicals Now, Renewal* or *Christianity* would serve this purpose. Sending a magazine as a gift subscription or perhaps forwarding one's own copies after reading them can be a real service.

Letters and tapes. There is nothing more maddening than the kind of letter that begins 'You will have heard all about such and such I expect, so I won't bore you with another account' especially when in fact nobody has sent any news about it at all. Two or three accounts of a church funeral or family wedding can be quite amusing in the way different people are impressed by different things. When we were in East Asia ourselves, Alan Stibbs, the busy Vice Principal of Oakhill Theological College, wrote to us every month, until he died, with news of things happening in the evangelical world. He had been a missionary himself, isolated in Inland China and knew how letters could help keep you in touch. We came to look forward to that neat rounded hand written

airletter coming each month. My mother-in-law was astonishing for the detail of her observations in her letters, so that
we felt that we were much closer to home and church, family
and friends. The arrival of cassettes of special family occasions that we could not attend, or of especially noteworthy
sermons given at church or at conferences were always a
blessing.

Remember that for the first five or ten years (!) missionaries
may not understand anything (to start with) or everything
(later on) at the church services they attend, and indeed may
not hear much preaching from anybody except themselves.
They begin with month after month of sitting in church services leafing through a dictionary in the hope of making some
sense of what is being said. During those years I used to read
one or two chapters of Alexander Whyte's Bible Characters
every Sunday afternoon, because there was no spiritual food
to be had from incomprehensible church preaching, and
while it was possible to sing the words of hymns, even then
poetic meanings were often obscure. The availability of cassettes can therefore be especially helpful for new missionaries
struggling to understand anything at all in church.

Music tapes and records. It is a real service when friends
keep you in touch with the latest good Christian music with
meaningful words – Kendricks or Dudley Smiths! But
remember that people can be blessed by good 'secular'
material also. As I travelled around visiting missionaries I
often used to ask how they relaxed. One most saintly lady
said she listened to Nana Mouskuri and read Georgette
Heyer novels. When I raised my eyebrows, she asked me
somewhat tartly where I thought unmarried lady missionaries were expected to get their romance from! Our children
introduced us to the Seekers, and other friends to Flanders
and Swann, and to 'The Driving Instructor' and other
sketches by Bob Newhart. We used to pass the best bits

round the field between us as friends so that others could enjoy it. A really good laugh with tears pouring down your cheeks, shaking with mirth can work wonders in those feeling downcast over lack of progress in the work. Sure, praying is better, but Scripture itself says 'a cheerful heart is good medicine'.[6] And as an additional tonic, humour and the quiet enjoyment of beautiful music is to be warmly recommended. A lively mission supporter, an American working for an oil company in Indonesia, said to us: 'Have you heard the Peanuts record? No? I'll send you one!' and she did. If you enjoy something, do not be afraid to share it with your missionary friends.

Telephone calls. I was recently visiting a missionary in Budapest, and was very impressed in the course of one evening, at the succession of telephone calls from family and friends at the other end of Europe. It was not just the content of the calls themselves, but the encouraging reminder that other people really have remembered us, that they are praying for us and that we have their friendship and support. That is so helpful. The callers knew when they might find their friend at home too. These supporters on the other end of the telephone showed that they were concerned, caring and close to the action.

E-mail. As I mentioned, a growing number of missionaries now have E-mail. Over the next few years we will see many more people in our own congregation with access to it. It may be worth a question in the church notice sheet to find out who has E-mail, and to pair up missionaries and supporters who might appreciate this very immediate (and very cheap) way of passing news both ways.

2B. Practical support when they are coming home

I had a letter recently about a missionary couple returning from Zaire. There was to be a welcome meeting for them in

August, then they would be giving a report on their work sometime in September. The point is that somebody had agreed that their home be used for both these meetings, and somebody else had planned these two occasions and sent out the letters. Every person serving overseas needs back-up like this: people who will fix things so that everything goes smoothly.

One time when we came home we found our house had been cleaned from top to bottom, the larder was full of freshly purchased stores and someone had even put tomato plants into our garden. We felt really welcomed and cared for and it made a great difference to our homecoming. 'Isn't it great to have a sending church like this!' we said to each other.

Recently a lady missionary from our church, returning for the final time from long years in Africa, was invited out, and on the way the group just dropped into the church – and, surprise, surprise, there we all were for a 'This is Your Life' style welcome home, with family, old friends and even some African friends there to be introduced in person, on the telephone, or with slides and pictures. Then we all ate a meal together. She was assured that her church loved and appreciated her, and would care for her as she came home. A whole team of people had worked together to make that possible.

Few missionaries, especially with growing children, can afford holidays in expensive resorts. We look back with thankfulness on friends who offered their holiday house in the Langdale Valley in the Lakes; a Free Church of Scotland minister who offered a locum in his manse while he was on holiday; a caravan by Lake Windermere made available free to missionaries; not to mention Swiss friends who offered holiday chalets in fabulously beautiful situations in Laax and Adelboden. Providing missionaries with a refreshing holiday break in the midst of what Thomas Valpy French called 'the vortex of deputation' can be a blessing indeed.

3. Prayer support

Prayer support involves much more than praying privately at home, or attending supporters' prayer meetings. Somebody has to organise such meetings, find a home willing to host them, prepare carefully so that they are well run, and so that people want to keep on coming back to them. A well run 'Supporters' Club' can be a spiritual force in the lives of those who participate. A badly organised one lowers morale and reduces a missionary's prayer support. Organising prayer meetings or a support group, sending out prayer letters, keeping up with changes of address, all takes time and care. There is a whole chapter later devoted to using prayer as a weapon in the spiritual battle.

Churches need more structures for prayer support. In 1950 the four hundred members of the Cambridge Inter Collegiate Christian Union, which had had a daily lunch hour prayer meeting since 1848, developed forty regional prayer groups of ten members each. These met four times a term or even weekly and involved the whole Christian Union. The group I belonged to prayed for Africa and more than half the group went to work there. Sadly this kind of commitment to missions fell off during the tumultuous sixties, though the early days of Operation Mobilisation brought a considerable revival of missionary concern.

I would agree that we had too many meetings in those days, and churches have to be careful to avoid endless proliferation of additional meetings, sometimes to deal with shortlived interests that then fizzle out. One of the best solutions seems to be to widen the scope of house groups and Bible study groups by making them responsible for praying for and communicating with particular missionaries or missionary families.

The widening distribution of *Operation World* is also helping to increase missionary prayer, and monthly facts sheets based upon it can do much to widen mission consciousness in whole congregations (see Chapter VII).

4. Financial support

For so many this has been the nitty gritty of sending missionaries. For some years in North America the late Oswald Smith galvanised churches into action with annual missionary fund raising using cash registers to tot up how much everyone was going to pledge to missions. It got people moving, but it became very easy to think that 'support' meant simply giving money: and I am trying to make the point that it is much, much more. Money is no substitute for other resources like human friendship, encouragement, time and trouble taken to help missionaries, and above all prayer for them. But we cannot ignore economics – travelling, housing, clothing, food and medicine all take money.

Yesterday I had a letter from Singapore describing the missionary giving of a group of Christian Brethren congregations. Of fourteen churches surveyed only one congregation was giving less than 20% of its total budget to missions, eight were giving between 20–29%, three were giving 30–39% and two were giving above 40% of their total income. This not only underlines the fact that missionaries are now coming from both the East and the West, but it shows how generous their home churches can be. Our home church here in Guildford gives more than 50% of its income to mission outside of the city.

(i) *How far ahead can we commit ourselves?* One of the problems for any church in screening and selecting potential missionary candidates and accepting them for support is getting the right balance. Accepting a long-term career missionary may mean committing the church to finding the funds for the next forty years. The attraction of very short-term missionaries from a budgetary point of view is that the church is only committing itself for one year or less, or even for a small fixed sum.

A married couple with children, who have to be fed, clothed and educated means finding several thousand pounds a year – not much less than any other similar family in the church would need each year: and in some countries of the world it costs considerably more than in Britain, especially when the exchange rates are unfavourable or the cost of living very high. It is always a good question to ask at church budget meetings: 'We have set aside such and such a sum for missionary family X. In realistic terms, how many months in the year are we actually supporting them for? And how will they eat for the other months?'

(ii) *How many months a year are we going to support them?* The same Singapore report commented that for too long missionaries were commended and sent out 'to trust in the Lord for their support'. While some congregations and individual friends were generous, some churches sent next to nothing. This is a misunderstanding both of the responsibility of the sending church, and of living by faith. The sent individual prays and looks to the Lord to supply all their needs – this is their faith attitude of dependence upon God. But there also needs to be a depending upon God on the part of the sending church: they also need to depend by faith and through prayer. When we pray 'Give us this day our daily bread' we are praying not merely for our own individual physical needs to be met, but for the needs of all the congregation, including those we have selected and sent out to be our missionary representatives. 'There were no needy persons among them' says Luke of the early church (Acts

4:34). It was a corporate support pattern. What we send to support workers overseas ought to be determined by their needs, and not by the limitations of the sending church's present budget.

(iii) *Are there limits to the number of people we can support?* Sometimes we may be anxious that there are limits to the amount that any one church can give out of its limited budget. This is not a groundless anxiety, especially for popular evangelical churches in cities with big hospitals, universities or (most of all) missionary training colleges on their doorstep. They cannot possibly hope to support every transient student who knows they are going to need support, still less fully support them all. Things are made more difficult when people join the congregation and then announce that their mission expects them to 'raise their own support' and that the suggested figure is so many thousand pounds a year!

One of the encouraging aspects of the increasing number of self-financing missionaries, who work professionally to support themselves, especially in countries which would not admit church financed missionaries, is that the so-called 'tent maker' does not need financial support, though he and she deserve all the other kinds of support in full measure. There is no limit really to the number of missionaries any church can support, if they do not need to call upon the finance budget! However, it is not quite that simple, for a salary for someone working in Bangladesh or China, for example, may only provide partial support and need supplementing by the supporting church.

However, we may ask the question whether it often happens that any churches are really over committed? Some churches have regarded tithing as mandatory, but others would say that if a tithe was demanded under the law, we should certainly not give less when we are not under law but under grace. Even so a church giving as little as a tenth of its members' corporate income should be able to support one Christian worker for every ten members. A small church in Tokyo, at a time when it only had seventy members, was supporting seven people full-time: the pastor and his wife, half of the support of a pastor and his wife in a daughter church; three students in Bible training and the total support of a Japanese lady missionary working in Taiwan. It seems unlikely that many of us are giving to our limits in giving to the Lord's work.

(iv) *Are there some causes which are more worthy than others?* This is a good question, and one often asked in North American books. There is a tendency to look for concrete results in terms of numbers of churches planted, bodies baptised and souls saved, but it would be foolish on that basis only to send missionaries to responsive fields. Eleven hundred million Muslims may not yet be very responsive, but God is glorified and seen to be great when the Gospel of the Lord Jesus is faithfully proclaimed among them.

Questions are always being asked about the proportion of income which is spent on home administration relative to the amount that is sent abroad. This is a good question to ask, provided it is recognised that retired missionaries need to be cared for, some children educated, some missionaries on home leave supported and that home staff members also have to eat.

There has been a recent tendency in some organisations to increase their real estate holdings, buying more and more property: and even going into debt and then putting an emotional pistol to all our heads. So we should not be afraid to ask hard questions, and listen carefully to the answers. It is noticeable that more and more mission agencies are moving out of expensive residential or city areas to cheaper parts of the country, and cooperating together to share the costs of offices and office equipment: this is good stewardship of

Christian resources. Those starting new missions of their own from scratch need to recognise that overheads are always relatively higher for small groups than they are for larger ones. Is it really totally impossible to find any existing like minded agency with whom they might work rather than starting all over again, and duplicating overheads?

There is a problem sometimes in getting the balance right between those working at home and those overseas, and even more between the number of short-term workers (especially when the trip is so brief it differs little from other people's recreational holidays!) and those long-term missionaries whose not inconsiderable support is a long-term call on a small church's missionary budget.

5. Outstanding models for the local church

I want to look at two churches: one present-day, and one eighteenth century.

Gold Hill Baptist Church is in the village of Chalfont St Peter in Buckinghamshire. It was built as a small country chapel, and, though still a member of the Baptist Union of Great Britain and Northern Ireland, has lost its strong denominational emphasis and draws in people from all sorts of church backgrounds, and from none at all. The church is situated in a residential area which has two council estates and a large number of private houses. Most people come from the immediate locality, but some travel in from other towns and villages.

Twenty years ago, the church had a membership of some 300. This has now grown to nearly 600 with perhaps 800 or so coming to events in any given week, and around 300 meeting for Bible study. A large youth section divided into eight age groups has around 400 on its books.

At the time of going to press, there were a total of fifty-four missionaries sent out from this church. The Mission

Council is alert to the congregation's need to be educated in world mission, and its responsibility to play a part in local evangelism, home mission in the UK, and overseas mission. The Council convenes three separate sub-committees to help in this task:

1. The Administrative Sub-Committee, to keep the profile of mission high in the church and among the youth organisations, produce literature, keep an up-to-date notice board, arrange occasional meetings, look after the house and cars available to missionaries etc.

2. The Members' Sub-Committee, to keep in regular contact with each missionary through one of its members, to ascertain special needs and make sure prayer news is fed back, to arrange valedictories, welcome homes etc.

3. The Candidates' Sub-Committee, to keep in close touch with all missionary candidates in training, and to give counsel to members of the congregation who are thinking and praying about service at home or overseas (including short-termers), then to make a final recommendation of acceptance to the Mission Council.

In 1990 Gold Hill gave away 33% of its annual income to mission, and aimed to increase this to 50%. By 1996, their giving had risen to 43% of the church's income.

Their mission policy statement[7] is carefully thought through and covers all matters relating to mission awareness in the church, training of candidates, pastoral care of people at every stage, and finance for their time of serving, and for after they retire. It also makes provision for young people to benefit from national and international conferences, which can be such an 'investment' in terms of spiritual growth and challenge. This policy statement is reviewed every five years to make sure it reflects the needs of the day.

The Gold Hill Prayer Diary is a simple but excellent production by a member of the Mission Council with access to desk top publishing equipment, and with help from people on the Mission Sub-Committees. It works through all the missionaries over the 30/31 days of each month, with a scanned-in photograph of them, a brief outline of their ministry, and an extract on their country of service from *Operation World*. Each missionary has a 'prayer support team', and the name of the leader(s) appears at the foot of page. This is straightforward to produce and highly effective in communicating needs.

The most outstanding local church in terms of mobilisation for world mission there has ever been was that at Herrnhut in Saxony, the mother church of the Moravian Brethren. A group of Christian refugees from Bohemia settled in the grounds of the home of Count Zinzendorf: their community became a remarkable local church, organised in 1727. In 1728 the single young men started a mission prayer group (sixty years before William Carey) and the first missionaries were sent out four years later, in 1732. By 1740 some 68 missionaries had been sent out from this one congregation, (that is about 8 people each year). By the time of Zinzendorf's death twenty years later in 1760 a total of 226 had been sent out from the one local congregation. The ratio of missionaries to members reached one in twelve! It shows remarkable commitment by one congregation to world mission. In a day when most Protestants still held a territorial view of the church under a Christian sovereign, as responsible only for their own Christian country, and under parochial restraints, this one local church started to feel a responsibility for the whole world.

Even more interesting was their method of selecting missionaries to send out. They had the concept of 'the whole church as mission'. Every single church member was willing to go if chosen. They would pray together as a congregation – and then cast lots – and those chosen would go! It was very prayerful church and they had a twenty-four hour prayer chain which lasted for over 100 years. Over 150 years they sent out 2000 missionaries from the one local congregation! The secret was that the whole congregation acted as a sending society, rather than mission being an activity for a few enthusiasts. It was also financially possible because these missionaries were all, of necessity, self-supporting, as channels for sending money hardly existed.

How do you respond to such a concept? Would you feel a bit anxious if your own local church started getting involved in such a thoroughgoing fashion? Or would you back it and support it and be thrilled if it did? Probably you feel both of these responses: but is there much doubt in your mind that such a church is more in line with the New Testament churches in Acts than most churches we meet today? Is this not a model for all of us to try to follow and implement in our own local church? If churches started to work and think together corporately about missions, then they might find it easier to work in the same way locally, and this would be a tremendous advance for many congregations.

Notes

1 *A Study of Fredrik Fransen: The development of his Ecclesiology, Missiology and Worldwide Evangelism* (Ann Arbor: University Microfilms International, 1985) p.318

2 Note Proverbs 30:24–27

3 Fredrik Franson (1852–1908) a man who in eleven years influenced the founding of ten different mission societies

in North America, Sweden, Norway, Finland and Switzerland. See Edvard Torjeson, *International Bulletin of Missionary Research, July 1991:* 'The Legacy of Fredrik Franson'

4 Hendrik Kraemer, *The Christian Message in a Non-Christian World* (London: Edinburgh House Press, 1938) p.41

5 James Paton (Ed.) *The Story of Dr John G Paton's Thirty Years with South Sea Cannibals* (New York: George Doran Co.) p.28

6 Proverbs 17:22

7 Reproduced in the appendix

CHAPTER III

THE ROLE OF PASTORS AND MINISTERS

The first professor of Mission in Germany, Gustav Warneck (1834–1910), lived out his whole life in a small area of Germany, without visiting any missionary situations whatever. He even sent learned papers to International Conferences without actually attending any of them! He had wanted to become a missionary but was prevented from doing so by ill health. I am not caricaturing German thoroughness when I tell you that he wrote a three volume work called *Missionsstunden* to inspire pastors and lay leaders of churches to promote a missionary spirit among believers in state churches. He said that:

> A sound and vitally active mission spirit with deep roots in the home church will always result from the fruits of sound pastoral teaching. Therefore, the pastor is the person in the best position to exert the greatest influence as a *missionary worker* in the homeland[1] (my emphasis).

I like Warneck's notion that the pastor is to be regarded as a 'missionary worker'. The attitude of the leading minister of a local church can make all the difference. It ought not to be left to visiting speakers to teach and enthuse a congregation about world mission. The person responsible for the majority of the teaching ministry ought to teach missionary responsibility and take a lead in developing it in the church as a whole. The pastor more than anybody else can encourage missionary concern to flower, or by his attitude can lead to the neglecting or even the stifling of it. We all know what a difference a new gifted leader can make in any congregation, in encouraging women's ministry or banning it, in developing evangelistic and church planting outreach, or concentrating on a pulpit ministry. It is difficult to do anything without the enthusiastic support of the minister, and he often is the one who initiates fresh developments.

Though the book *Ten Sending Churches*[2] has been out of print for some years now, one of the most striking things about those churches was that in nearly every case the church only fully awoke to world missionary concern after their minister's own interest had been aroused. This is understandable in any church. In anticlerical churches like the Christian Brethren who discourage one man ministry, if the elders are sympathetic, or enthusiastic about mission this will have an influence on the congregation, as a whole.

1. Pastors Speak from their Own Experience

It seems sensible therefore to use not so much my own words and experience in this chapter, but that of ministers of churches and their own experience in leading their whole congregations into deeper involvement in mission.

Malcolm Widdicombe of St Philip and St Jacob, Bristol (better known as Pip and Jay's) was unusual in seeing world missionary responsibility as part of his original call to the home ministry, through reading Oswald Smith's book *The Challenge of Missions* when recovering from flu. That interest was well fostered during his five years of training for the ministry at what was then Tyndale Hall, Bristol,[3] the training college of the Bible Churchman's Missionary Society (now Crosslinks). This underlines the importance of including some stimulating teaching on mission for all ministers in training; it is sadly true that few denominational colleges include mission in their syllabus, or have a professor of mission on their faculties.

Even in colleges where mission studies are included in the curriculum, they may be one of many options available, and some may study little if anything about mission. It may not seem immediately relevant, but if a church is going to send out missionaries, it is essential that the person pastoring understands their pastoral needs. Malcolm Widdicombe's personal target was that the church should give away more than they spent on themselves. In 1964 missionary giving was £64, by 1969 it was £1840 (more than half of their church income then) and by 1983, almost £68,000. Yet he is eager to say 'we never resorted to money-raising efforts'[4] because the focus was on what they were seeking to achieve rather than money. Speakers like Harry Sutton helped to get them excited, but clearly it was Malcolm's own commitment that encouraged the church to become increasingly involved. Most of our churches are organised in such a way that the minister who leads it can have a huge influence for good and growth, or for stagnation and inertia.

Jim Graham, who has now been followed by Stephen Gaukroger at Gold Hill Baptist Church, was invited to minister to missionaries in East Asia, and his enthusiasm for mission has, under God, helped to make what was already a thriving church into one with a worldwide concern. (It now supports over 50 missionaries.) He admits quite frankly, 'Until the last twenty five years the church's attitude to and involvement in mission was dutiful, traditional and denominational – like the majority of churches throughout the United Kingdom.'[5]

This all began to change, and you can understand why when Jim writes: 'Mission needs to be removed from the periphery of the church's life and put at the heart of our life together. Involvement and responsibility have to be moved from the 'enthusiast' to the 'ordinary' church member. This was achieved – at least in part, because we have so much ground yet to possess – firstly teaching the principle of mission and evangelism regularly, consistently and clearly from the Word of God.'[6]

Jim helpfully summed up by quoting Douglas Webster as saying that 'we need to make the local church aware of the total church.' In other words, this is a consciousness-raising exercise. To state that goal is simple, but to achieve it requires a great deal of persistent, hard work.

Tom Walker, formerly vicar of St John's Harborne in Birmingham, then Archdeacon of Nottingham, and now retired, wrote of the leave which St John's gave him to visit members of the congregation serving in South America:

'It is true to say that the vicar was more in need of a sabbatical break than the missionaries concerned needed pastoral attention, but the tour gave a sense of mutual responsibility in God's work. Returning home, it was evident that the visit had an enormously beneficial effect in subsequent prayer backing, and in knowing how to decide matters of practical help.'[7]

Again it is clear that opening the eyes of the minister to the actual needs of churches overseas was decisive in getting the church launched into mission orbit. The minister is so often the first stage rocket that enables the church as a whole to take off. If the leader is something of a damp squib, the consequences are not impressive!

Barrie Taylor, formerly minister of Alton Evangelical Free

Church and now World Mission Secretary for the
Evangelical Alliance, wrote most frankly:

'The problem was not so much that there was no mission
interest in the church . . . one tenth of the church's income
was given to mission . . . there were to be found in the church
some missionary prayer warriors . . . The problem right then
was in my own heart, a heart cold towards mission, lacking
in biblical perception, vision and zeal in this vital area.'[8]

He added, 'Little did I know that I would soon visit Africa.
The word "sabbatical" is like music to any pastor's ears, and
the church in Alton made that a reality for my wife and
myself in giving us a four month break. This gave me the
opportunity to respond positively to the invitation of SIM to
visit, as one of their council members, the missionaries in
West Africa.'[9]

He was challenged by a young Liberian Christian who
was acting as his interpreter, 'Just five words that went like
a sword to my heart, making me wish the ground would
open up and hide me.'[10]

Those five words were the simple question 'What is your
mission strategy?' But that started him searching the
Scriptures afresh and reading books about mission. At a
joint elders' and deacons' retreat they met to examine their
response to mission.

'God met with us that day and we were conscious of his
mercy towards us amidst all our shortcomings and failures.'
Following that meeting Barrie observed, 'The over-riding
need was to educate biblically so that the church might see
that mission was rooted in the word of God, felt in the heart
of God, and carried out by the Spirit of God through men
and women in the hands of God. The preaching, taking the
form of systematic exposition, now drew attention to
mission theology and application. Formerly these aspects
had been neglected.'[11]

Barrie tells of the impact made on him when the young Liberian believer spoke of the help he needed if he were to become a teacher of God's word.

'I thought of all the hoarded spiritual resources back home in the United Kingdom, my heart melted, and a tear reached the veranda floor . . . my heart welled up, my throat tightened around the lump forming in it, and through my closed eyes came a trickle of hot anguished tears.'[12]

We appreciate Barrie's frankness. Even a Bible-loving church and its committed leader could be sadly lacking in mission vision, until the Lord stepped in to convict and bless them all.

2. Others Speak of the Pastor's Key Role

Underscoring the ideas of the Scots missionary Alexander Duff (1806–1878) Gustav Warneck declared, 'the greatest obstacle to the advancement of world mission lies in the indolence and apathy of pastors.' Such radical thinking was unacceptable to most German pastors of his day but being a pastor himself Warneck could speak from within the circle.[13]

At a significant conference of British missionary societies held in Liverpool in 1860, J B Whiting, a secretary of the Church Missionary Society, spoke graphically of the important role of the church minister: 'We must fan the flame of missionary zeal in the pastor. Can an icicle light a fire?'[14]

It is something that every individual minister needs to ask of him or herself: can it be that my lack of positive enthusiasm and encouragement for mission means that men and women who ought to have gone out from our congregation have not gone, that missionaries have suffered from shortness of supply through my own failure to press home the needs on the congregation? Have I perhaps damned the work of missions with my faint praise? Scripture commands:

'Obey your leaders and submit to their authority. They keep watch over you . . .' but also adds the words, 'as those who must give an account'.[15] And we shall all appear before the judgment seat of Christ to give that account in relation to the world mission of the church.

In contrast to that disappointingly negative view of the minister's role, contrast it with the enthusiasm of Jim Graham:

'I well remember one of the most dramatic church meetings I have ever been part of, when, as a Fellowship, we were convinced that if God would honour us by calling men and women out from our church to serve him, we would be responsible to supply the resources, both spiritual, material and financial to maintain them in the ministry to which God would call them. Excitement mingled with faith in the light of reality!'[16]

A most interesting example of the extraordinary influence a pastor may have upon a missionary was that of Campbell Morgan, for many years minister of Westminster Chapel and a noted Bible teacher, and his influence upon Miss Mildred Cable, who was for forty five years a missionary supported by Westminster Chapel. *The Westminster Record* in January 1907 printed a letter from an unknown missionary in China requesting church membership. She had spent her student years studying chemistry, and the biblical teaching she had received from Campbell Morgan during his ministry at Tollington Park laid the foundation for her own teaching ministry.[17]

When the Friday Bible School started, she saw it as crucial for her future overseas service, and she entered wholeheartedly into it, adding hours of private Bible study to her ordinary studies. She thrived on the intense analytical study as they covered a whole book each week, and then themes, gaining in a year a deep knowledge of the whole Bible . . .

Campbell Morgan supported her application to the China Inland Mission: 'I have never recommended anyone for missionary service with more wholeheartedness or stronger conviction of fitness.'[18]

In 1908 after her first term of service in China (seven years in those days), Mildred Cable was introduced to the congregation by Campbell Morgan: she was not then the eminent, famous explorer she became later. She was to be a member of the chapel for forty five years. She drank in the teaching given at the Friday Bible School sessions at the Chapel. The new Women's Bible School building in Huozhou, Shanxi province, contained a plaque commemorating a gift from Westminster Chapel.

The Trio (Misses Cable, Eva and Francesca French) returned on furlough again eleven years later in 1920. They had done a superb work, providing first a boarding and day school for the education of Chinese girls and subsequently a Bible School for Christian women. Those they trained became Bible Women and Women evangelists, pastors' wives and were in demand as teachers in new government schools. In spite of twenty years work in education, at forty-five Mildred with the French sisters (both in their early fifties) felt called to return to evangelism in the far North West of China – Gansu, and the old Silk Road across Xinjiang. Mildred turned to her pastor for wisdom and guidance. She said later that he had followed all that she was doing in China with the utmost interest:

> and when I had to make a decision which entailed leaving the work in North China . . . to take an unknown path that was going to lead me across the dreary wastes of the Gobi Desert, he understood the depth of my need for guidance, and he was full of understanding and sympathy. He was one of the few who grasped the sense of urgency which was upon me.

What a model of pastoral concern and encouragement! Campbell Morgan was a busy minister of a large church with a substantial teaching programme, but he made time to relate to the missionaries sent out by the church. In a letter to Mildred Cable found in his biography he writes as follows:

> You will understand with what intense interest and sympathy I have read your letter . . . It has been given to you to do a great work in these twenty-one years, and I am perfectly certain you cannot lay it down without some sadness . . . You must in such a case rest in the assurance that the One Who is calling you out to a new venture -or I would rather say adventure – will not fail to guide and govern in connection with the work which you now lay down. You certainly are being called to one of the difficult outposts of the field, and I think you are justified in looking upon such a call as a high honour conferred upon you by the One Who is directing all the affairs of His own work in this world . . . I need say no more on the subject, for I am certain that you and your fellow workers know the place you have in my heart and thought and prayer.[19]

It is clear that many, many people in that distant part of the world were to benefit from the example set by Campbell Morgan. J O Fraser visited the area as a CIM Superintendent and he reported back to Shanghai: 'I don't suppose we have in the whole of the CIM a more capable teacher than Miss Cable – of any subject. She was recently offered a position in the Shanting University. The thoroughness with which she teaches Dr Kao's young men [and women] is almost appalling! She makes them go through the whole Bible – no skipping – Minor Prophets, Revelation, everything. It is remarkable that whereas so many of us common missionaries have been more or less satisfied with a superficial knowledge of the Bible in our Chinese Christians, here –

right up in one of the remotest corners of China – you have a band of young men who are being grounded in the word of God as very few others are in any part of the country.'[20]

You can see at once the influence which Campbell Morgan had upon this member of his congregation, and the extraordinary degree to which this influence was extended to the far reaches of China. A pastor's well prepared teaching ministry can achieve great things for God, when they give a model of teaching which can be adopted to different situations in other languages.

Mildred Cable was a member of Westminster Chapel for forty-five years until her death at the age of seventy-five. Campbell Morgan died in May 1945, not long after VE Day. At his memorial service chaired by Dr Martyn Lloyd Jones, Mildred Cable spoke of what Campbell Morgan's ministry had meant:

The 'contagion' of Dr Morgan's enthusiasm for Bible study had changed the lives of many of Christ's ambassadors . . . As I talk to you now I can see Bible Schools in Central Asia where thirty men and women have given up their time for the winter months . . . the textbook is the Analyzed Bible in Chinese [authored by Campbell Morgan]. We missionaries have lost one who has been to us a teacher and a friend; one who sponsored all our work with prayer and with thought; one who always wrote strong words of encouragement when we needed them; and whenever we committed words to print we always received appreciative letters from him . . . speaking for myself I can say that I caught from him that which has been my passion through life, to know this Book by every translation which I could buy, every language in which I could read it, to study it in and out in every way.[21]

Mildred Cable was not the only CIM missionary to benefit, for it seems that it was customary for CIM missionaries in training at Newington Green to attend

Campbell Morgan's Bible School on Friday evenings.
Campbell Morgan longed to see a full time Bible College
established in London, and though he was by then too old
and frail to bring it to fruition, many of those who
founded London Bible College were friends and associates
of his.

Notes

1 Gustav Warneck, *Missionsstunden*, (Gutersloh, 1878–1897) c.113

2 Ed. Michael Griffiths, *Ten Sending Churches*, (London: MARC Europe, 1985)

3 Amalgamated with Clifton Theological College, and Dalton House to become Trinity College, Bristol.

4 *ibid* p.32

5 *ibid* p.49

6 *ibid* p.53

7 *ibid* p.114

8 *ibid* p.121

9 *ibid* p.128

10 *ibid* p.120

11 *ibid* p.123

12 *ibid* pp.121–123

13 Hans Kasdorf article in *Missiology*, July 1980

14 Conference on World Mission held in Liverpool p.60

15 Hebrews 13:17

16 *ibid* p.52, 53.

17 Valerie Griffiths, 'The Teachers of Righteousness', *The Westminster Record*, 1995

18 *ibid* p.1

19 Jill Morgan, *A Man of the Word: Life of G. Campbell Morgan* (London: Pickering and Inglis, 1951) p.358

20 Eileen Crossman, *Mountain Rain: A new biography of James O Fraser*, (OMF/Harold Shaw), p.199

21 Jill Morgan, *A Man of the Word: Life of G. Campbell Morgan* (London: Pickering & Inglis Ltd. 1951) p.324

CHAPTER IV

THE ROLE OF FRIENDS AT HOME

Much that has already been said about the sending church applies to a wider circle of Christian friends who may not belong to the sending church. We may have met them first in Christian service activities like beach missions and camps, at Greenbelt or Spring Harvest, perhaps in Bible College and missionary training. We may have met at conferences of mission supporters, who promised to pray and will indeed do so. Probably we meet many that we would like to have as friends, but the pressures of modern life prevent us having enough time to spend with them so that we can bond together as friends. Sometimes frustrated by lack of time to spend with friends, or even to read all those annual letters that arrive at Christmas, we realise how much we need heaven in order to spend more time with one another and relish our friendship to the full.

1. Biblical Models of Friendship

Old Testament Models

Abraham is called God's friend,[1] while 'the Lord would speak to Moses face to face as a man speaks with his friend.'[2]

The relationship of God to both Abraham and Moses is expressed in terms of the intimacy of human friendship.

The friendship of David and Jonathan became proverbial. It was marked by Crown Prince Jonathan's generosity as he admired the courage of this youngest son of a country farmer:[3]

> Jonathan became one in spirit with David, and he loved him as himself . . . and Jonathan made a covenant with David because he loved him as himself. Jonathan took off the robe he was wearing and gave it to David along with his tunic, and even his sword, his bow and his belt.

The Book of Proverbs includes some significant comments about friendship:

'A friend loves at all times, and a brother is born for adversity.'[4]

'A man of many companions may come to ruin, but there is a friend who sticks closer than a brother.'[5]

'The kisses of an enemy may be profuse, but faithful are the wounds of a friend.'[6]

'As iron sharpens iron, so a man sharpens the countenance of his friend.'[7]

When we are away in a far country, to be able to write and open our heart to a personal and trustworthy friend, is a blessing indeed. In the reverse direction, the arrival of a letter from a friend lifts the heart and assures of that sense of solidarity and support that strengthens the heart. Alan Stibbs's monthly letters, which I have already mentioned, did that for us for many years when we were living in East Asia.

New Testament Models

The Lord Jesus was a highly sociable person, relating to all sorts of people across the social spectrum. He is contrasted with the ascetic John the Baptist,[8] remaining out in the desert. So well known is his capacity for friendship that he is criticised for it in that passage as 'the friend of tax collectors and sinners'. He may have retired to pray on his own 'a great while before day', but the picture we have of him is surrounded by people all day long. There are no less than seven dinner parties in Luke's gospel, and Jesus is a popular after-dinner speaker. The wedding at Cana shows him astonishing with the quantity and quality of his generous gift, that saved the face of a family in danger of disgrace in failing in hospitality before the whole village. Instead of gibes about Stingy Simon or Mingy Menachem, for years afterwards people would remember that they had never tasted wine like that before or since. The presence of this highly sociable and attractive person, the man Christ Jesus, brings joy to all who meet him.

It is clear that in addition to his choice of the Twelve, and sometimes of a chosen three from among them to accompany him, he also had a wider circle of those who are called his friends. 'Jesus loved Martha and her sister and Lazarus'[9] we are told, and he seems to take especial pleasure in visiting them and eating with them. But the Twelve most of all he treats as friends, and exhorts them to treat each other as friends.

> Love each other as I have loved you. Greater love has no one than this, that one lay down his life for his friends. You are my friends if you do what I command. I no longer call you servants, because a servant does not know his master's business. Instead I have called you friends, for everything that I learned of my Father, I have made known to you . . . This is my command: Love each other.[10]

There is a close relationship in Greek between the various words for love and for friendship. Christ is not only our closest friend, but commands his followers to give that kind of committed friendship to one another. As we develop such bonding between us as Christian friends, we are obedient to the command of our Lord.

It is remarkable how frequently words for 'friend' and 'friendship' crop up in the letters and ministry of the apostle Paul. In Ephesus some of the council of the Asiarchs were his friends.[11] When the ship bound for Rome on which Paul was held prisoner, stopped at Sidon, the centurion Julius allowed him to go ashore to see his friends.[12] The word friendship is used for the relationship that developed with Publius of Malta.[13] We often think of Paul as a somewhat rugged, self-sufficient personality, but it emerges that he has a huge warm Jewish capacity for friendship: he is, to use a Jewish phrase 'a real mensch!'

The last chapter of Romans is remarkable in a letter addressed to a city which Paul had never yet visited: he knows no fewer than twenty-six people there by name, of whom nine are women. Indeed he actually calls some of them friend: Epenetus, Ampliatus, Stachys and the woman Persis[14] are all, one after the other, singled out as 'friends'. This man has built up a network of friends all around the Mediterranean, and he keeps in touch with their movements. Elsewhere in his letters six others are described in this same way: Timothy;[15] Tychichus;[16] Epaphras;[17] Onesimus;[18] Luke;[19] and Philemon.[20] I find this impressive and compelling: this man knows how to make and keep friends. But he uses other words that express a sense of relationship: in the letter to the Philippians he speaks of having the same soul,[21] and later calls Timothy a 'kindred spirit'.[22] If we have expounded the command of Jesus to his followers to love each other as a command to build a network of friendships between the members of the Christian community, then Paul provides us with a wonderful illustration of precisely that.

Christians are not expected to be maladjusted, socially autistic loners, but are commanded to demonstrate that warm capacity for human friendship that we have seen illustrated in the Scriptures.

2. Models of Friendship from Missionary History

Charles Simeon, Vicar of Holy Trinity Church, Cambridge was able to recommend five of his assistant curates and proteges as chaplains to the British East India Company at a time when missionaries were still not permitted to enter British India. (Carey, Marshman and Ward resided in Serampore, which was a Danish colony, when the British refused them entry.) These 'Famous Five' were all highly significant in the progress of the Gospel in India, which then included what is now Pakistan. When David Brown, who had become a Christian at Holy Trinity, was sailing for India in November 1785, he recorded in his journal that Simeon not only came to see him off from Tower Bridge, but on the next day astonished him by appearing on board at Gravesend, where he had ridden over 'in order to give his adventurous young friend a second farewell.'[23] Simeon himself was only twenty-six at the time, and had been vicar of Holy Trinity for three years, but even so riding on horseback from Cambridge to the mouth of the Thames involved a great deal of trouble. They continued to correspond for the twenty-five years that David Brown laboured in the heat, stench and pressures of Calcutta.

Robert Louis Stevenson was originally somewhat negative about missions: 'I had conceived a great prejudice against missions in the South Seas, and had no sooner come there than that prejudice was at first reduced and then at last annihilated. Those who deblaterate against missions have only one thing to do, to come and see them on the spot.'[24]

This change of heart was the result of an encounter Stevenson had in 1890 when travelling on a German ship the 'Lubeck' to Samoa from Sydney, New South Wales, when he met up with a fellow Scot, the missionary James Chalmers, of the London Missionary Society. The weather was rough and they spent the time swapping stories in the smoking room.

'Chalmers was a man after Stevenson's own heart. Then he was a fellow Scot, and had for twenty-five years been living through and experiencing adventures by flood and field of the very kind which possessed the most attraction for the author . . . Nor was Stevenson slow to recognise and reluctant to acknowledge the value of the friendship thus begun.'[25]

He referred to him as 'the man I love', and Stevenson hoped to visit Chalmers in New Guinea. This was unhappily impossible, but they did correspond, Stevenson calling himself 'Your affectionate friend'. He wrote: 'I am a man now past forty. Scotch at that, and not used to big expressions in friendship; and used on the other hand to be very much ashamed of them . . . I count it a privilege and benefit to have met you. I count it loss not to meet with you again.'[26]

Chalmers's biographer wrote concerning this friendship: . . . 'for Mr Chalmers, Tamate of New Guinea, he felt a kind of hero worship, a greater admiration probably than he felt for any man of modern times except Charles Gordon.'[27]

When Alan Stibbs was working in Szechwan with the China Inland Mission, he and a fellow Englishman, Theodore Benson, would walk thirty miles just to meet together, pray and encourage each other. One thing to pray for any missionary is that they may have friends, not only among their fellow missionaries and other expatriates, but with national Christians. It is this bonding across cultural boundaries which is so needful for effective service, and which becomes not only a channel for the Gospel, but a crossbeam which strengthens the Church of Jesus Christ.

3. How Does all this Work Out in Practice for Missionaries Today?

Missionaries need a double circle of friends: their old friends back in their home country, and their new friends on the field, national Christians and international colleagues. It is true that good missionaries are those who make friends of national believers, and bad ones are those who fail to establish friendships. Friendships back home are very significant, as it is such teams of friends who will give moral and logistic support and encouragement, and above all pray.

We have to be realistic about the pressures of modern life also: not everyone in the sending church can be in a close support relationship, for an active sending church may have sent out several missionaries and therefore different members will feel drawn to support one person more closely than others: this is perfectly natural and proper. It also underlines the fact that in addition to a good sending church everybody also needs a support team of people who feel personally committed to help, and pray for a missionary couple or individual. They may not be able to support very much financially, but that does not matter very much: it is the caring and the praying which really matters.

There is a most evocative parenthesis from Paul in writing to the members of the local church in Thessalonica. 'But brothers, when we were torn away from you for a short time (in person, not in thought)'[28] or as the NRSV 'in person, not in heart' and the Good News Bible 'not in our thoughts, of course, but only in body'. Paul is recognising what every mother knows, that being separated geographically in no way reduces caring concern, and that even at a distance one can feel intense anxiety and love for people who may be out of sight, but are certainly not out of mind. This capacity for caring at a distance, and praying from a distance is essential in supporting front line Christian workers in cross cultural situations.

The most fortunate missionaries are those with a substantial circle of sending friends, a team of praying people, a kind of Supporters' Club who may never meet each other, or may meet together at regular intervals. The important thing is that support is there – not only when the missionary individual or couple are at home, but also in their absence. Three examples:

Sandy is one of the most friendly, outgoing people I have ever met. He was at Oxford University, lived at the Kilburn Club,[29] went on to study at London Bible College, then learned colloquial Arabic in one Middle Eastern country and was expelled for his evangelistic activity. After some time in Egypt he is now working elsewhere in the Middle East. He and Kirsten married after meeting in Egypt.

They are both letter writers and would like to write personally to all their supporters, but content themselves with a quarterly prayer letter. Both had built up wide circles of friends, scattered from one end of Britain to the other. It is not easy to keep up with them all. On this last home leave they travelled widely visiting old friends. They let all their supporting friends know where they would be speaking, so that those within reach could get to see them. Kirsten had arranged books with maps, photos, artists pictures etc. to explain their area of work, in a looseleaf folder, so that they could be pinned up on walls as a kind of exhibition. Their supporter's club is very widely spaced, and that made it difficult to get everybody all together, but they covered a lot of ground last summer.

Chris and Lucy studied at London Bible College for one year each in consecutive years, while the other worked to support the family. Their support group consists of people from their supporting churches, friends they made at

London Bible College, and OMF supporters generally. They worked first with OMF in Hong Kong, where they learned Cantonese, and were considering moving to Vietnam, where that language is still widely spoken. Subsequently a business invited Chris to run their computers, so that having started as a language-learning missionary, Chris and Lucy have become self-supporting workers using their business experience. They have a well organised 'Supporters Club' to stand behind them: for they need just as much prayer support as they did before, when first going cross cultural.

Andrew is a man of considerable experience, having worked as a teacher, as a UCCF Travelling Secretary and assistant pastor at Above Bar Church, Southampton before going to London Bible College, where he was elected Student Chairman and gained first class honours. He then went to work in Austria as an IFES staff worker attached to the national Austrian student movement OSM. After some years he was invited by the Baptist Church in Innsbruck to become their pastor, a real compliment to any expatriate and his linguistic and spiritual abilities. He sends regular letters in a somewhat unusual and well integrated format to a wide circle of praying friends.

All of us need supporting groups behind us like this.

Notes

1 2 Chronicles 20:7; Isaiah 41:8; James 2:23
2 Exodus 33:11
3 1 Samuel 18:1–4
4 Proverbs 17:17
5 Proverbs 18:24
6 Proverbs 27:6
7 Proverbs 27:17 KJV
8 Matthew 11:18–19

9 John 11:5

10 John 15:13, 14

11 Acts 19:31

12 Acts 27:3

13 Acts 28:7

14 Romans 16:5, 8, 9 & 12

15 1 Corinthians 4:17

16 Ephesians 6:21; Col.4:7

17 Colossians 1:7

18 Colossians 4:9

19 Colossians 4:14

20 Philemon 1:3

21 Philippians 2:2 *sumpsuchos*

22 Philippians 2:20 *isopsuchos* that is literally 'same soul' or perhaps 'soul brother' in contemporary idiom.

23 Hugh Evan Hopkins, *Charles Simeon of Cambridge*, (London: Hodders, 1977), p.143

24 Graham Balfour, *Life of Robert Louis Stevenson*, Vol. 2 p.193

25 Richard Lovett, *James Chalmers his autobiography and letters*, (London: R.T.S, 1903) pp.352–3

26 *ibid* p.396

27 Balfour, *ibid* Vol.2. pp.126–7

28 1 Thessalonians 2:17

29 The Oxford Kilburn (OK) Club is a social and evangelistic work in North London founded and supported by the Oxford Inter-Collegiate Christian Union (OICCU).

CHAPTER V

THE SUCCESSIVE STAGES OF THE CHURCH'S ROLE

1. How Does a Local Church Select and Train Missionaries?

The Church plays its part but we must recognise the role of the Chief Harvester in what is happening: it is the Lord himself who is active in the lives of his people. But at each stage the local church and its leadership must consciously act as the Lord's agent in the selection process.

2. How the Lord Works to Guide Us Through Our Local Churches

In one sense the growth of Christian workers within the life of the local church is a common sense affair: this is what actually happens, but the one who makes it happen is the Lord himself. I want to stress the work of God through his Holy Spirit. Churches and their leaders may either actively promote the church's mission through their enthusiastic teaching, and establishing of priorities, or on the other hand they can passively stifle it.

1. *Involving us*: The Lord gets us involved in Christian activities. Our local church asks us to take responsibility in the Youth Fellowship, to teach in Sunday School, or to speak at a women's meeting. Our local church is the nursery in which all of us are trained and shaped for good or ill.

2. *Inspiring us*: The Lord gives us the Spirit's presence and help in serving and speaking. 'I never would have thought I could have done that,' people say. But the Holy Spirit helps us, giving the words and the way to express ideas. When I was eighteen years old, I was invited to give a ten minute talk at a wartime Bishop of Rochester's Harvest Camp, and I can still remember that sense of God's Holy Spirit helping me.

3. *Inviting us*: The Lord prompts our local church and its leaders to invite us to serve and speak. These opportunities enable us to grow. Churches need to be giving opportunities and experience in church work to their own members, who are potential mission workers. 'One man band' churches of the traditional style are not very good at this.

4. *Introducing us*: The Lord arranges for us to meet overseas workers. They may have been invited by the local church in the first place, or by those organising conferences. In God's sovereignty he causes us to meet people who become significant models and mentors for our lives. Meeting those already involved in mission helped shape people like Mark and Timothy. It is still the most significant factor in helping individuals move towards mission. When I was still a schoolboy, Alan Stibbs (then recently returned from China) and Bill Butler (working in East Africa) filled such roles for me. As students, we were privileged to have many such models.

5. *Informing us*: The Lord quickens our interest in particular work in particular places. This may well happen through meetings organised by the local church. Or through

our buying and using *Operation World* from a church bookstall. Or through reading Christian biographies and books on mission.

6. *Impelling us*: The Lord himself impels us to take positive steps, while we consult and pray with our local church and its leaders. A relaxed interview with prayer, with an elder or our pastor, is an important first step for many of us.

3. Christian 'Staff Development'

The Lord's selection and training takes place as the local church is discipling all its members generally. How good to remember that 'Nothing that you do for him will ever be lost or wasted.'[1] But there does also need to be some deliberate process of identifying members' spiritual gifts. The leaders (elders, deacons, missionary committee) need to take time to recognise developing gifts, and to create more opportunities to develop people's gifts further. This requires more than a cheerful, nonchalant assumption that everything will turn out all right in the end, whatever we do. It requires a proactive concern for every church member and a desire to develop each one to their full potential.

This kind of 'staff development' is now built into most progressive businesses and educational institutions. However churches have been passive and very slow to recognise that this is a biblical process for developing the gifts of all our local church members. You can ask members to tell you what they think their spiritual gifts are and then give them jobs to do, but this can be a very mechanical exercise unless it is accompanied by creative prayer that the Chief Harvester guide us in matching people's gifts to roles which are calculated to widen their experience and develop them as Christian workers.

4. How Does a Local Church Help Screen Potential Christian Workers?

Screening is essential. Not everyone who is willing to go overseas, or who thinks they have a call, should be encouraged to go. They may be too young and need to be told to wait. They may have family responsibilities for ageing relatives they must not shirk. They may have health problems they have to live with, or personal or family histories of mental stress, which may mean they should not be put under increased pressure. They may be unsuitable because of temperament, personality or lack of gift. Every elder of the Korean Presbyterian Church stood to their feet in 1912 to indicate their willingness to go as missionaries to Shandung Province in China. All of them were willing, and that enabled the church to sort out those who were most suitable. Not all who are willing and available are called or suitable, even when they think they are.

Does this sound unspiritual? What happens when an unsuitable person is encouraged to go abroad? Perhaps they crack up after a few months, or become easily discouraged. One missionary society asks the questions on a pre-home leave report: 'Is there a welcome back from the national church? Is there a welcome back from fellow missionaries and is there a welcome back from the field leader?' One might survive a negative to the second and third questions if they were the only contrary voice: they rarely are. Such people may hang on for three or four years, but finally their fellow missionaries have to tell them sorrowfully that there is no welcome back: their gifts 'would be better deployed at home'. However nicely that is put, everyone understands the real message: 'You have failed: you are not able enough for this task and we do not think it worthwhile keeping you here!'

Frankly, it is cruel to expose anybody to that sense of failure. It may take months or even years to get over, and some people never get over it. It is not only the individual who suffers, if that were not bad enough: the people who sent them out feel bad, and sense that their stewardship of church funds has been ill advised. The national church at the receiving end feels let down. Why did they send us someone who had so little to contribute? Surely his home church must have known his limitations and weakness? And fellow missionaries feel let down because instead of a colleague to help carry the load, they were sent someone who became a hindrance rather than a help.

When we screen inadequately, cherish naive expectations, and stifle the doubts and hard questions, we expose people to unnecessary failure. Churches know candidates much better than missionary agencies do at the application stage. They fail in their duty if they do not act with wisdom, discernment and discretion. We must not unload our oddballs, loose cannon or doubtful starters on the churches abroad.

A local church, which has known its members over an extended period, is better placed to assess a person's potential usefulness than a missionary society interviewing panel. Selection conferences and committees only see people on their best behaviour, concerned to make a good impression. Church leaders soon discover whether people are content to sit passively in the pews or take initiatives. Bible and theological colleges also see people over a more protracted period, and daily rather than once or twice a week, so may often be better placed even than churches to recognise the strengths and weaknesses of students. However I have found that in colleges we can become attached and committed to our students, and so may have an exaggerated view of their potential. A readiness to discuss and combine their experience and expertise is highly desirable for no selection method is foolproof. Objectivity is always difficult.

Screening is not easy. The Lord's hand may be upon people who at first sight seem less gifted and able. When we first went out to Asia, one of our much appreciated fellow new missionaries used to weep every time she failed to get her service over the volleyball net. But she had extraordinary courage, and kept on coming back again and again. Nothing deterred her. She never was much good at volleyball, and she did not have the academic record of some of us: but she was still in action thirty years later, in pioneer situations, travelling alone in far away places, and a radiant person it was a blessing to meet and be with. Fortunately those who screened were not misled by the outward appearance, when she seemed shy and nervous.

At the opposite extreme was a man with advanced degrees, manifestly clever, showing great language aptitude in language learning. But his wife broke down after six months. They have both had very significant ministries since, though I wanted to weep as they told me what it felt like to arrive home returning as 'failures'. They were great people in the wrong place. Some who look like bad risks turn out wonderfully, and some who look like a sure thing disappoint everyone including themselves.

We must do our utmost to reduce to a minimum those who have to bear that unbearable sense of failure. We should not do it to one another. It brings our guidance under question, it makes those we misguided question the goodness of God, and it troubles the church of God and shakes the confidence of fellow missionaries.

Screening then must be thorough. It must not depend on people who do not really know the candidates, but those who have lived and worked with them over a sustained period. Nor can it depend upon over-optimistic people: one

Bible College principal was notorious because all his students were given glowing reports – with the result that if he said the least negative thing about one of his protégés, we dropped them like a hot brick!

We must needs scrutinise physical and mental health, as well as security and mutual respect in marriage relationships. How have they been appreciated by employers and colleagues? The secular viewpoint is often most revealing. Do even their most loyal friends have some doubts about their suitability? If they really feel called to Africa or China, have they sought out and made friends with African immigrants or Chinese students in this country? If they really are called to mission, have they made time to attend a missions prayer group?

Over the years I have noted that when a student at college or a missionary on the field fails in some way, if you look back at what their referees had to say when they first applied, there is almost always an indication of some weakness. But the scrutinisers ignored it when they met the applicant for a relatively brief interview, took a liking to them, had a hunch about them, and ignored the comment of someone who had known them longer.

Screening is tough: and we can agonise over it. Members with experience over several years get better at it and learn from their mistakes. Selecting the selectors in a church is very important. If a church expresses doubts, the missionary agency must take notice. If a training college expresses doubts, the sending church must take it most seriously. The threefold sieving process provided by local church, training college and missionary society should serve to filter out most of those who ought not be sent. Any one of the three could make a mistake in discerning God's will, but they complement each other. A college forms relationships, thinks the best and does not want to downplay its own products; a local church may favour a large frog in a small pond; and a missionary society may be too eager for reinforcements. So praying to the Lord about screening and selection is so important.

There is a huge value in the objective guidance of others. All but the overconfident suffer from some measure of self-doubt (and they are not safe missionary candidates anyway!). The individual needs a sense of assurance that God is calling them, but at the same time we know that people can deceive themselves: so perhaps I can deceive myself too. And it is in that circumstance that other people's far more objective view of us can be so helpful: some of us have too high a view of ourselves, and many of us have too low an opinion of ourselves. It is here that the objective guidance of a whole group of other people can be so helpful in confirming (or even throwing doubts upon) the reality of our subjective sense of call.

5. How Does a Local Church Support Members in Relating to Missionary Agencies?

In our individualistic culture, members of our churches are often left alone in approaching missionary training colleges and missionary societies. Both those bodies will require letters of recommendation from the church leaders, but this is a very passive form of church involvement. How much better when such applications are made after full discussion between, and prayer with, the church leadership. It can be a huge help if people know that the church is behind them, believes the time is right for them to take the next step, and supports their choice of college. Their approach is then supported by people who believe they have already shown gifts and fruitfulness in Christian service. A firm promise of total or partial financial support is further evidence of their backing. The College then knows that here is someone that other people are behind, and think worth training.

It really helps if the church continues to show interest. They could pray for those in training, and consult and counsel with them at regular intervals. They could visit the college and see it in action for themselves, and give the person a real sense that they are not in some academic limbo, but living active members of their local church. How are they getting on with studies, with their teachers, with balancing their individual budgets, and with their practical training? If they are married, does the spouse feel isolated, or part of the college fellowship? Is the marriage under stress, because one of them is in training and the other is only marginally involved? A closer relationship between churches and the colleges training their students enables these questions to be addressed.

The support of the church is even more true of application to a mission agency. There must be some objective confirmation from a fellowship of believers, who know the people well, and are prepared to recommend them to the society. The church's conviction about the call of the individual is further confirmed by their willingness to back them financially.

The sending congregation needs to be involved with the mission agency from the beginning, and a cooperative relationship established between them. They are not some disinterested party, handing over the person to the society, and washing their hands of them. The mission agency is only a channel facilitating the sending church in sending out missionaries, by using its expertise and experience of the foreign situation, a knowledge which few local churches can hope to possess.

6. Sending and Laying On of Hands

Laying hands on missionaries before sending them out is a time-honoured biblical procedure. 'So after they had fasted and prayed, they laid their hands on [Barnabas and Saul] and sent them off.'[2] The precedent goes all the way back to Moses and Joshua. 'So the Lord said to Moses, "Take Joshua, the son of Nun, a man in whom is the Spirit, and lay your hand on him. Have him stand before Eleazar the priest and the entire assembly and commission him in their presence. Give him some of your authority . . ." then he laid hands on him and commissioned him.'[3] 'Now Joshua, son of Nun, was filled with the Spirit of wisdom, because Moses had laid his hands on him.'[4]

The procedure was used also from the earliest days of the Christian church, so that when the church had selected the seven men, and presented them to the apostles '[they] prayed and laid their hands on them.'[5] The Seven were commissioned for a ministry within the Jerusalem church, but with the laying of hands in Antioch, Barnabas and Saul were commissioned for a ministry elsewhere. They were set apart for that ministry, commissioned and sent out under the authority of that congregation. And later, when Timothy was to accompany Paul and Silas,[6] hands were laid on him both by the elders of the church in Lystra[7] and by Paul himself.[8] In both verses this is seen to bear relation to the spiritual gift of teaching given to Timothy.

When commissioning a married couple, it is important to lay hands on both husband and wife, and if children are involved, to pray for them also.

This practice is a solemn and responsible thing for the church to do, an outward visible sign of its commissioning and sending of individuals and families. Saying farewell to people at railway stations and airports is good, but nothing is as good as the solemn commissioning of those who are being sent, by those who are sending them.

Professor James Stewart, the great Scottish preacher, described to me the huge impact of several hundred Scottish students bidding adieu to Eric Liddell, the Olympic Gold medallist, as he left Edinburgh for China. I find one never forgets the friends who took the trouble to come and see us off.

7. How Does a Local Church Support their Members Working Overseas?

We speak here not only of 'missionaries' in the traditional sense. With the increasing flexibility and width of present day options, many churches have members who are working and witnessing overseas, who may be supporting themselves financially. They are in just as much need of moral and prayer support as those whom the church is helping to support financially.

We have already treated this at some length in Chapter II, where we concentrated on the different things people could do to help and support. The local church needs to exercise oversight over all of that: to ensure everything that can be done is being done, and nothing is being left undone, and keep the channels of communication open, so the whole church can have a sense of participation in the trials, troubles and triumphs of their missionaries.

The pastor and elders must see themselves as pastorally responsible, even if they delegate the 'nuts and bolts' to the church missionary committee. Such committees are not acting instead of the church and its leadership, but on behalf of the church and its leadership. There may be occasions when direct telephone hookups are possible, so that the voice of the missionary can be heard speaking to the congregation during the course of a Sunday service – that can be moving indeed. But there may be issues that perhaps are not appropriate to share with all in public, but need to be handled quietly in private. Showing that the church cares, and wants to hear, is very important.

Notes

1 1 Corinthians 15:58 (Phillips)
2 Acts 13:3
3 Numbers 27:18–23
4 Deuteronomy 34:9
5 Acts 6:6
6 Acts 16:1–3
7 1 Timothy 4:14
8 2 Timothy 1:6

CHAPTER VI

SNAKES AND LADDERS: THE STAGES OF A MISSIONARY'S DEVELOPMENT

The experience of cross-cultural Christian workers can be a pattern of changing stresses. Supporting churches need to be aware of this and to be conscious of where counselling and friendship are most needed. It is easy for us at home to think of those who are sent out as a homogeneous group not realising that people will have very varied experiences. This reflects not only the variety of cultures and situation in which they may be working, but the individual Pilgrim's Progress through a series of occupational hazards. It could be compared with an emotional switchback, or even the game of Snakes and Ladders!

1. The Waiting Years – Uncertainties and Patience

Initially they want to go out right now: why bother with training? Some school leavers are all keen and committed to go now, today, and somewhat crestfallen when one does not seem equally enthusiastic. The average age of new missionaries going long-term is approaching thirty. To have something to offer at the other end they will need experience of working in a local church, and Bible training or theological training, as well as cross-cultural training. Architects, doctors, psychotherapists, engineers and lawyers all need professional training over a number of years and missionaries need it too. At the same time I would always encourage them to find ways of getting abroad sooner rather than later, and not to dilly dally on the way. The younger someone arrives overseas, the easier it is to learn language and culture, and to bond with brothers and sisters in Christ in the other country.

Later on, so many are the hurdles put in their way, they begin to wonder whether they will ever get out. They will need wise and experienced counselling during this stage. Some will have unreasonable expectations as to how quickly they can be prepared for overseas work: and some unwisely grab at short-term options precisely because they make fewer demands for training and experience. Some who at one stage seem committed to go are deflected by other career possibilities or by potential life partners who do not share their goals.

They themselves may experience a change of interest and focus: I all but went overseas to train children's evangelists in East Africa (on the strength of beach mission experience, chiefly). But church planting began to seem more significant.

Missionary societies at first seem so welcoming, and 'come hither', but once interest is shown, start asking all manner of complicated personal questions, suggesting further training possibilities, and they may seem to take far too long to make up their minds. They require medical examinations and even psychological testing, and their procedures often seem tiresomely cumbersome to the uninitiated. The society needs to work out which national church at the receiving end has a welcome for the potential candidate. Finding a place where the varied gifts of husband and wife may both fit is not always so simple: once a theological lecturer married to a doctor applied. They were highly gifted people – but there was nowhere to be found in that country where a theological college was situated close enough to a hospital that needed a doctor!

Churches need to appoint people as mentors to keep in touch with church members passing through these difficult years of waiting and preparation. There are so many possible slips between the cup and missionary lip! Many difficulties are placed in people's way: sometimes by the enemy opposing them, sometimes by the Lord testing their willingness and commitment: and people need experienced Christian counsel and encouragement during this time.

2. The First Few Months – Euphoria

How long this lasts depends on the person's temperament! It may disappear on the plane out as they begin to wonder how on earth they ever got themselves into this situation! It may disappear if they experience sharp culture shock. We knew one lady who found herself the only woman on a plane full of Muslim men. She was dressed very discreetly, and humbly entered the plane last. However the man in the seat behind put his feet over the back of the seat on which she was sitting, with his smelly socks by her face; it was quite deliberate harassment. By the time she arrived she was, not surprisingly, in acute culture shock. At the opposite extreme some very unusual people may remain in a state of euphoric bliss on Cloud Nine more or less permanently.

The best kind of preparation for cross cultural mission, given by colleges specialising in missionary training, can do a great deal to minimise both culture stress and anti-climax.

If you know how bad it can be, you are favourably surprised that it is really not that bad at all! If valedictory services provide an encouraging 'upward ladder', there is some inevitability about the 'snake' bringing them down again once euphoria wears off!

3. The First Couple of Years – Language Study and Frustration

The church is waiting for reports of great exploits and multiple conversions, and all you have to write about is irregular verbs! Few people at home realise how much time has to be spent in language study by those who need to be fluent enough to preach Christ effectively in a foreign language. Mercifully most missionaries tackle one language at a time, though some countries may demand both a national and a tribal language. Thomas Valpy French once gave this advice to a newly arriving missionary:

> You must, of course, commence with Urdu or Hindustani, so as to be able to talk with your servants, to help in the services of the church and in the schools. You had better give some six or eight hours a day to that, and also spend two or three hours at Punjabi, to be able to talk with villagers. You should also try to give two or three hours to the study of Persian, which you will find invaluable in the schools, and all your spare time (*sic*) to the study of Arabic, so to be able to read the Qur'an.[1]

If that does nothing else, it should convince you that new missionaries immersed in language study need prayer. Few probably realise how inadequate is the language of a first term missionary: as short on vocabulary as any incoherent teenager. It's easier to talk in gospel clichés translated directly from your own language and set phrases, than it is to give a clear, reasoned talk on the death of Christ, or a persuasive presentation of the Gospel relevant to a different culture.

Those who have been active Christian workers can find it very difficult when they can't communicate in a foreign language. Most newcomers fail to realise most ordinary people speak no language but their own, and find it almost frightening to come up against the blank wall of irritated incomprehension. It is the loss of identity, role and respect which really hurts. One friend wrote saying that having been respected as head of a computer firm, now he was just an ignorant alien, reduced to baffled lack of comprehension! This was true even among Christians in the church fellowship – having been an elder in his home church, he was now merely a stupid embryo missionary unable to communicate even on the simplest everyday matters. It is an utterly frustrating experience: some less well-prepared people have deliberately isolated themselves from useful ministry, and suffer a kind of reversion to infancy and babbling incoherence.

Being born again into a new culture means that, like all babies, you can only communicate by smiling. And while that can show human warmth, and desire for friendship and relationship, it is not always easy to keep smiling when one feels so frustrated. It is a bit like the agony of a stroke victim, when they have lost the power to speak, and then have to relearn it through struggling misery. It may not be physically so difficult, but the frustration is almost as great. And the more gifted and the more effective a Christian worker has been, the greater the sense of deprivation from loss of ministry. If people have not been well prepared, this is where some people do give up and throw in the towel.

Careful screening for 'stickability' is so important. Those with a history of instability and failure to persevere need to be screened out, for everyone's sakes and not least their own. One really does have to be willing to fall into the ground and die, in order to grow up again into a fruitful worker.[2]

4. The Next Couple of Years – Growing Confidence and the Beginning of Fruitfulness

Those first two years can last a long time. You have nothing spiritual to write home about (you cannot write too many letters about irregular verbs) and after years of fruitful Christian activity, even the most outgoing person passes through the utter frustration of having a forced vacation. It is almost like being in prison, and isolated from all you enjoy doing. But slowly progress is made, though the speed differs from person to person. (That is what Modern Language Aptitude Tests are supposed to be measuring after all.) But almost everybody makes some progress, and the tortoises catch up with all but the most gifted hares.

The effect of this is that though the tunnel has seemed very long, there is light at the end, and the light gets brighter and brighter as the months go by. How useful any first-term missionary can be depends upon (a) the relative difficulty of the target language. For example Indonesian language learners start to communicate much more quickly than those studying Arabic, Cantonese or Korean; (b) the person's aptitude; (c) the spiritual passion and dependence on the Lord of the individual, and perhaps also (d) having people around with some ability in the missionary's native tongue, like English-speaking Africans, Indians, Singaporeans or Filipinos.

There is always some recognisable progress, and the dawning realisation after months of frustration that perhaps one is going to be useful after all! However as the time comes for home leave, and all the excitement of reunion with the sending church, with parents, brothers and sisters, personal friends and old acquaintances, one must stop the work in which one has just begun to be useful.

5. The First Home Leave – Loss of Role

Home leave used to be called furlough, which sounded like a holiday, when it wasn't. While it may have included some initial holiday, it was mission-directed time. 'Furlough' has rather disappeared as an outdated colonial word, and now been replaced by 'home-leave', 'home-assignment' or similar words.

It may come as a shock to realise that return to what used to be familiar surroundings, and happy reunion with home church, family and friends is not glory, glory all the way! It's like making a bad throw in Snakes and Ladders and you shoot down to another emotional low. There are many good and understandable reasons for this, though churches oddly are often the least able to grasp how disorientated the returned missionary can feel.

(i) *Loss of a permanent home*. A few may be able to return to their own house, but many will be temporarily housed in rented accommodation, or staying in a house with family or friends. Chinese wisdom uses the pictograph of one woman under a roof as expressing 'peace and tranquillity'. Sharing roofs and kitchens can be a trial to the sanctification of most wives and mothers. When we arrived home for the second time, having spent the previous leave in my wife's parents' home (I was away preaching a great deal and it didn't worry me), I could not understand at first why she was in tears and desperate for us to rent a place of our own. The grandparents found it difficult to understand also, but both we and our children really needed space and time together.

(ii) *Children born overseas feel disorientated*. When our children have been born overseas, what is home to us is a

foreign country to them. Our children at first thought eques-
trian statues in London to be evidence of idol worship!
Another family's children enjoyed themselves flushing every
toilet in the house until they got used to this novel form of
sanitation! And small children may have to enter a strange
kindergarten or primary school where they know no other
children to start with. They may not be understood even by
teachers: 'You have an odd child,' one teacher told us. 'He
keeps on slipping out of his shoes under his desk and
however many times I tell him to put them back on, he still
seems to prefer to have them off!' In Japan nobody is so dirty
as to wear their shoes in the house, and the poor kid resented
being forced to wear shoes indoors!

If the house is being shared with parents or parents-in-law,
the children suddenly find that they are receiving additional
instructions on behaviour from two more adults, whom they
do not know very well, not having grown up with them.
Moreover their parents seem oddly distracted and spend all
the time talking to people who are total strangers to the children. If the children are disturbed by their new and strange
surroundings, then this can upset the parents as well.
Mercifully children often seem more adaptable to changing
circumstances than their parents are!

(iii) *Missionaries can feel unemployed*. They have always
had a regular job to do in their home country before: now
they appear to have none. Overseas the missionaries had just
begun to develop a useful role, but now they have come back
home again, they suffer a further loss of identity. In terms of
their home country, they seem almost to be unemployed, and
have no role that is easy to understand. Their job is thousands of miles away, and though they are expected to go
round talking about that job, they are removed far from it.

(iv) *They may have no role in their local church either*.
Earlier they may have been members of church committees,

or leaders of church activities. Now they are 'Our missionaries home from abroad,' but they have no role. They hopefully have been publicly welcomed back, and in a good
church may even have enjoyed some kind of welcome
meeting at which they gave some account of their work, and
were affirmed by the church. But usually they have no satis-
factory role in it for the time they are at home.

In a small church, if they are very gifted they may even be
perceived as a threat by the minister, but more usually it
never seems to occur to anyone that being theologically
trained, they are at least as well qualified as other members
of staff to minister the Word of God to the church. They will
perhaps be asked to show slides at some poorly attended
midweek meeting, and if they are asked to speak it will be to
speak about their work or about missions. Here are potential colleagues and fellow workers, who could reinforce the
work, pioneer new outreach and be a blessing to the
congregation. The church selected them to go overseas
believing they could be a blessing to other people, but oddly
it never seems to occur to even the most well meaning
Christians that they might also be a blessing to them too, if
only they were given the opportunity.

This would be a biblical way of using missionaries. For did
not Paul and Barnabas minister in their home church of
Antioch on their return from the first missionary journey?
'Paul and Barnabas remained in Antioch where they and
many others taught and preached the word of the Lord.'[3] If
the missionary is a single woman, her case is often little
better, and can be very much worse. The missionaries must
console themselves with the thought that even the Lord Jesus
said that a prophet was not without honour except in his
own country. Excluding missionaries from ministry in their
own home congregations certainly contributes to a low sense
of self-worth and increases their disorientation.

There are some glorious exceptions to this sad pattern where everybody all over the rest of the country is supposed to want to hear these missionaries minister, but their home church gives them little or no opportunity at all. One missionary serving in Hong Kong is an elder of his home church, and remains an elder even when serving abroad, and takes up his responsibilities when he returns home. He really does have a recognisable role in his home church. Other churches regard missionaries as members of the church staff who are serving abroad, and welcome them back as members of staff, who attend staff meetings and are given useful work to do with their home congregation. This can make all the difference to giving identity and meaning to returned missionaries. Sadly this is more often the exception than the rule!

Many missionaries on furlough are oddly disorientated, and their sense of isolation is increased by their treatment at the hands of their home churches rather than diminished by it. At the spiritual level, there is an extraordinary failure of pastoral care, and at the human level, a lack of ordinary common sense imagination and sympathetic understanding! Once the missionary has been sent by a local church, they rarely get an opportunity to minister to the very people who recognised their gifts in the first place. It seems totally stupid, but so few people seem to recognise this problem.

(v) *They are expected to engage in 'deputation'.* This is the practice whereby missionary societies expect their members to visit many other churches in order to speak about their work. It needs to be re-examined and certainly modified, if not abandoned altogether. The need for fund-raising is part of the motivation for this practice, and that may be the result of lack of realism in levels of missionary support from the churches. Of course, the need for other churches to gain the widest possible picture of the worldwide church is also true: few churches have sufficient missionaries of their own, or a wide enough spread geographically to see the whole picture. Of course then, they need to have the opportunity to hear what the Lord is doing in many other parts of the world. It would not be good if there were no such visits at all, but the interests of the missionary must also be taken into consideration.

What are the less helpful results of deputation? For the single, frequent absences from base can increase their sense of rootlessness. They come home very conscious that many of their old friends are married and have homes of their own: because they have been called to missionary service, they have none. It adds to this sense of impermanence if you are expected (as single women in New Zealand did) to spend weeks away from home, speaking in different churches night after night, rarely in the same bed two nights running. Though less disorientating for the married, constant absence of husbands from home makes it harder for wives, themselves needing extra support because of their own sense of alienation, and it is not good for the marriage or for the children if they see too little of the husband and father of the family.

Lack of imagination or opportunity for service in one's home church, and the expectation of large numbers of meetings in other churches, can be damaging.

This is perhaps more negative than it needs to be, and an increasing number of churches and ministers are trying to be more thoughtful and considerate. To state it positively: the caring, sending, church must do its utmost to provide a clearly defined role for missionaries on home leave. They need the opportunity to do what they have been deprived of doing for the past several years: ministering the Word of God in their own native language to an encouraging and sympathetic audience. The church needs to enable them to be active Christian workers again, after several years when lack of language and then limited language has severely restricted their fruitfulness. Surely they could be given the chance to do something more than show slides and talk about the work they are no longer doing?

Involve them in the home church that sent them out. This can be a liberating experience for them, and will raise their morale to new heights. Instead of feeling 'I was not able to be much use overseas in my first term, and I was even less use when I went back to my home church', they will be reinvigorated with a fresh sense of call. Needless to say this problem is most acute for missionaries on their first home leave. Failure to return to the field may in some cases be as much the result of failure of the home church to reactivate the missionary, as to lack of sense of call in the missionaries themselves. Do you see how crucial is the role of the sending church and its leaders in this regard? You have the responsibility in local church leadership to convert a potential downward snake into an encouraging upgoing ladder!

There is a huge need of sensitive pastoral care for returned missionaries. On the field they are too busy to reflect much about their lives: but in this prolonged period of relative inaction they start to realise, possibly for the first time, what they have sacrificed in leaving a well paid job in their own country, for a poorly paid job overseas. Is this the time to change back again before it is too late? Anxiety about schooling for the children deepens, perhaps away from home in boarding schools even at primary school level: it works for some, but not for others. What will it be like for our kids?

6. The Second Term of Service : Liberation!

Returning overseas to a country whose language you can now speak, albeit imperfectly still (language refresher courses after home leave can be a real benefit), is utterly different from the miserable frustrations of the first term spent to some extent incommunicado. If home leave was a snake, this is definitely a ladder that raises the worker to new heights on the board. If home leave has been disappointing (and in the past, it has been for many), something can be done by wise debriefing by field leadership. 'How did it go? Was your home church helpful? Through whom did you get the greatest blessing?'

You cannot undo the results of neglect by the home church, but you can perhaps ameliorate them a little by giving a listening ear. But the dark tunnel now lies behind, and increasing fruitfulness should now lie ahead. Some countries are difficult: those in lands where church growth is slow or those working in Muslim lands, where church growth is minimal, need the greatest support. Here clearly, we are not talking about money, but of moral support and encouragement, the knowledge that your support team at home is rooting for you, and most of all labouring in believing prayer for breakthrough, for significant conversions, for committed disciples, for gifted national workers and for church growth – not only numbers but quality. The missionary is now becoming increasingly competent and can communicate the word of God in terms understood by the host culture. This is the opportunity for the support team to revel in the work and indeed to share in it through their prayers. This emphasis is so clear in the New Testament. (See Chapter VII).

7. Second and Subsequent Home Leaves – Turmoil

The workers now return, mature and experienced, and having been fruitful. The failure of the home church to give them any meaningful role can still produce a sense of loneliness, alienation and even a feeling that everybody is so busy living their own lives that they are not really interested. The returning worker is likely to have been overworked and comes home this time exhausted and spiritually dry like a squeezed out toothpaste tube. This is likely to become more acute as people take on more responsibility and leadership overseas. Each home leave is therefore different. They may need a great deal of rest and recreation before they embark on any ministry. The need for sensitive pastoral care and significant friends is as great as ever, the more so as other problems are beginning to arise, which tend to use up a great deal of emotional energy and dominate their thinking above everything else.

(i) *Education of children.* If the children have already been in school abroad, it may well have been a small mission primary school with dedicated and loving staff. The transition to the rough hurlyburly of an ordinary secular school, with the possibility of bullying and cruel teasing, can be traumatic for some kids. Quite apart from getting children into strange schools, whose structure and methods may be different from field schools, for the time at home, the question of their long term education begins to loom large: will they return to their home country for secondary education and if so will it be day school or boarding school, and where will they be housed, and where will the money come from? Or will they be educated in schools abroad in Africa, India or the Philippines? Quite apart from the problem of how all this will be funded, there is the question of whether parents and children can face the separation necessary to enjoy secondary education in the English language.

(ii) *Maintenance of the missionary call.* Years ago I heard David Bentley-Taylor give a seventeen point address and one of them was this: 'It's difficult enough to leave home the first time, but it becomes harder and harder each time you have to go back.' Well-meaning family and friends often suggest that now one has done one's bit, it is time to settle in back at home. So all these issues surface. Should the parents continue overseas or stay at home while the children complete their education? But this is the parents' time of maximum fruitfulness overseas, and what employment would they be able to find at home after ten or more years' absence from their home country? Are they qualified to be anything other than a missionary now?

Worse, it is quite possible that father and mother are not in full agreement about what they should do anyway. They really need not only pastoral counselling, but career counselling as well. And what about their sense of call? The sense of rootlessness and disorientation that is so common among missionaries on home leave makes decision-making harder, and skilled counselling all the more necessary. But do normal pastoral and career counsellors really understand, and do even church leaders understand? Often they do not seem to. These problems can be less acute for professionals overseas, because their time overseas may even enhance their chances of employment (though not always, by any means, if they have stepped off a professional ladder).

(iii) *Health problems.* This is probably less acute than in the days when most missionaries had survived life-threatening illnesses, or came back with livers loaded with amoebic cysts, debilitated by hookworm and other parasites, suffering recurrent bouts of malaria and so on. It is much less common to meet unhealthy missionaries nowadays: they often seem more healthy than those who have stayed at home with their allergies and stress syndromes! But hepatitis remains an occupational hazard in some areas, and wives may have suffered more miscarriages than normal, or have chronic anaemia.

Missionaries are no less liable to fall ill than other mortals, and they too suffer various stresses, and home leave is one of them, as I have tried to show. People who have been fit on the field when they were busy, often fall ill at home when they are not so busy! They suffer feelings similar to the unemployed. Really good and thorough medical examinations by someone who knows something about tropical diseases shortly after return from abroad is essential so that any persistent symptoms may be treated and the causes eliminated. Some countries have special clinics that specialise in such medical check ups, but doctors in local churches, with overseas experience, and time and interest to give, can be a real blessing.

8. Resettlement

Recently a whole book has been written on the problems of settling back into one's home country.[4] When the missionary comes home, several issues arise:

(i) *Housing*. Unless they were able to buy a house before they left in the first place, this will be their chief need. Even if as young people they once had savings, those are usually used up in paying for missionary training. Some will sell a house, if they had one, in order to pay their fees. Certainly on missionary incomes most will have little or no life insurance and very little in the way of savings or pension provision. In this regard their position is much like ministers except that churches reckon to provide housing for their staff. In some cases there may be family money that has come in the form of legacies. Some churches have provided housing for retired couples, and singles. I look back with pleasure to a retired missionary who had worked on the Thailand side of the Mekong River for many years, saying: 'Come and see the lovely flat my wonderful church has found for me.' It is a remarkable illustration of God's faithfulness that so many missionaries are provided for, either by family money, or by the generosity of churches.

(ii) *Employment*. If they are already of pensionable age, they may not need to find employment, but if they have decided to move back home for children's sake, or reasons of health, in their forties or fifties, the question arises as to what they will do next, and how they will be supported. Those with theological training may well qualify for a pastoral role as ministers, team members or in a church as an experienced lady worker with a great deal of experience to offer (and this may solve the housing needs). Some may serve on the home staff of their missionary agency, or find work with some interdenominational society.

Doctors, nurses and paramedics can usually find work, though sometimes not without re-training. Part-time or supply teaching may help until teachers can find a full-time post. But in days of high unemployment, finding suitable work especially for the less obviously gifted may be a problem. The problem can be more acute with some of the short-term missions where young people join without any accredited theological training, stay on more permanently and then find themselves in their forties with a family, and with no recognised qualifications whatever. Young people need to be advised by their churches of the possibility of this problem arising.

While churches cannot be expected to act as employment agencies, pastoral support and counselling will be needed, especially during the frustrating period when nothing seems to be happening and they wonder if they will ever be able to find work as rewarding as they enjoyed overseas. Returned workers suffer all the problems of other unemployed people. 'Tent makers' hopefully will not find it so difficult to find work related to their professional skills. After years of living simply but on a more or less regular income, it can be humiliating to find yourself on the dole: even committed Christians need pastoral help and encouragement at such times.

(iii) *Financial support.* While retired workers may receive a state pension, they may not have very much besides in the way of savings, insurance policies or pension provision. Missions may have some kind of retirement arrangements within their means, but the local church may feel responsible to help out in situations of need. The self-financing worker usually has few problems here. However, this does depend on where he was working and what he was doing. If he was struggling on a salary while having to pay for children's education in another country, the story may be different. We have to recognise that pension prospects vary from mission to mission. Some societies have comprehensive, transferable pension plans. Some undertake to pay National Insurance contributions, thus enabling their members to claim a state pension which the society may or may not choose to supplement. Others make no pension provision whatsoever. (At the moment, government policies – in the UK at least – are throwing increasing doubt on the validity and sufficiency of state pensions.)

As for 'tent makers', professional workers in more developed countries will be able to live on the salary paid. Others, in poorer countries, will almost certainly not.

Those intending overseas service, while prepared to step out in faith, should sensibly make an informed inquiry before leaving these shores.

(iv) *Church related ministry.* Where a church has been responsible and given missionaries a ministry as members of a church staff team during periods of home leave, there may well be a place for such an experienced and valued worker to work part-time or full-time on the staff of their home church. It is certainly a possibility which a church should always consider. I know of a Baptist church in North London which not only provided ministry opportunities for missionary couples on home leave, but also provided a place on the staff and subsidised housing when they returned home permanently.

What I have tried to do in this chapter is to show that missionaries are ordinary people, not supermen and wonderwomen clothed in impenetrable armour and spiritual asbestos. Their work puts them under particular stresses, not least when they are back on home leave. It is tragic to debrief a worker arriving back on the field, as I have, after they have been back with their home church, and ask: 'Well, how did it go? Did you have a good time back at home?' and get the reply, as I once did, 'Do you really want to know the truth? I have never felt so lonely before in my whole life.' She had felt marginalised even by her home church.

There is a role here for a Supporters' Club, and for church members to provide ordinary human friendship, warmth of welcome, hospitality and a listening, sympathetic ear. But the continuing care of long-term missionaries needs to be thought out carefully and imaginatively. It can be heartwarming and give a deep sense of security when missionaries know that they have a home church that really cares for them and sees them as much more than an item in the church budget!

Notes

1 Herbert Birks, *Life and Correspondence of Thomas Valpy French, First Bishop of Lahore*, (London: John Murray, 1895) Vol. 1 p.47

2 John 12:24

3 Acts 15:35

4 Peter Jordan, *Re-entry: Making the Transition from Missions to Life at Home*, (Seattle: YWAM Publishing, 1992).

CHAPTER VII

PRAYER FOR MISSIONARIES IN DAYS OF DISTRACTED BUSYNESS?

While all of us give lip service to the importance of prayer for missions, in practice many are too busy to give it much priority. We would protest that we care, but that others are praying, and surely God himself will watch over his servants and bless their work, and so that leaves me out. Even if we spend time reading the Bible, often our prayers are more focused upon ourselves and our family's needs, than they are focused upon the church as a whole. We may pray for our own local church, but fail to develop world wide ranging prayer. A brief chapter does not allow scope to write about prayer at length, but our focus is upon prayer for the church worldwide, and for worldwide mission.

So why should we pray?

1. Praying is Biblical

In nearly every one of his letters, Paul asks for prayer for missionary activity, urging them to pray for Barnabas, Silas, Timothy and himself. In most of his letters he begins by praying for those to whom he was writing. While this could be said to follow letter writing conventions, Paul transforms cultural traditions by infusing them with new meaning: and nearly always at some later point he urges them to pray for him. Paul's exhortations to join in prayer do not date: they are still relevant.

> *Romans 15:30* 'I urge you brothers by our Lord Jesus Christ and by the love of the Spirit to *join me in my struggle by praying* to God for me. Pray that I may be rescued from the unbelievers in Judea and that my service in Jerusalem may be acceptable to the saints there, so that by God's will I may come to you with joy and together with you be refreshed.'

Paul expresses it like this because he believed that it was possible for others to participate in his ministry by praying. He uses a compound word beginning with *sun-*, as in symphony, synthesis, sympathy that means to do something together with others, in this case 'wrestling together'. The same root word is used of Epaphras in Colossians 4:12, but without the prefix *sun-*. See what is being said here. Though removed from the scene of action, the 'sender' may join the ones 'sent' in their struggle by praying.

> *2 Corinthians 1:10,11* 'On him we have set our hope that he will continue to deliver us, as you help us by your prayers. Then many will give thanks on our behalf for the gracious favour granted us in answer to the prayers of many.'

This raises issues of our conviction and faith: do we really believe that we can actually assist in work taking place thousands of miles away by praying for it? This conviction is essential, but it needs to result in positive action and not be left in the realm of theoretical belief.

> *Ephesians 6:18–20* 'And pray in (*by means of*) the Spirit on all occasions with all kinds of prayers and requests. With this in mind be alert and always keep on praying for all the saints. Pray also for me, that whenever I open my mouth, words may be given me so that I will fearlessly make known the mystery of the gospel, for which I am an ambassador in chains. Pray that I may declare it fearlessly as I should.'

This much neglected section follows on the famous section on the armour of God and the description of spiritual warfare. If preachers only expound the items of armour these verses may be omitted. Neither we, nor our first century Christian ancestors, dressed up in literal armour to contend with spiritual forces of wickedness. The armour is the illustration. These verses are the explanation of how Christians may actually 'fight' in the real world: by praying, first for all the saints, and so for the national fellow Christians who the missionary works alongside; and also for the missionary ambassador himself, in need of courage and boldness. I recollect being with a senior worker, who would always hesitate before opening his mouth in the Open Air Meeting: we are timid mortals most of us. Like the early church, we need to pray for boldness.[1]

> *Colossians 4:2,12* 'Devote yourselves to prayer, being watchful and thankful. And pray for us too that God may open a door for our message, so that we may proclaim the mystery of Christ, for which I am in chains. Pray that I may proclaim it clearly as I should . . . Epaphras who is one of you and a servant of Christ Jesus, sends greetings. He is always wrestling in prayer for you, that you may stand firm in all the will of God, mature and fully assured.'

Paul prays for *opportunity*, without which there is no chance to communicate, and *clarity*, so that the opportunity is not wasted. And he cites Epaphras as someone who truly wrestles in prayer on their behalf.

> *1 Thessalonians 5:25* 'Brothers pray for us,' the most terse and briefest of requests.
>
> *2 Thessalonians 3:1–2* 'Finally, brothers, pray for us that the message of the Lord may spread rapidly and be honoured, just as it was with you. And pray that we may be delivered from wicked and evil men, for not everyone has faith.'

If you have any doubts about this need for protection, consult CEEFAX Travel News and see what a perilous world we live in. We need to pray with persistence for the gospel to spread rapidly, and with understanding of the problems our missionaries face. They are still part of our local church 'body' and we can work through them and alongside them through our prayers.

> *Philemon 22.* 'One thing more. Prepare a guest room for me, because I hope to be restored to you in answer to your prayers'.

Paul expects all Christians to get involved in mission, sharing in the same struggle, through praying. He does this in days before the availability of photographs, slides, telephones, cassettes or even a regular mail service. Other travellers had to carry news, money and letters from place to place, either on foot along the roads, or by sea on relatively slow moving boats dependent upon wind or oars. Nonetheless Paul expected Christians to share with him in the work of mission through their prayers. How much easier it can be for us today with all the aids provided by modern technology.

2. Praying is Human

It's human to care about your friends. Mothers and grandmothers carry photographs of children and grandchildren in their handbags. But now the extended family of the church needs also to express its love and concern for absent members of the body. We're back to Paul's delightful comment to the Thessalonians: 'But brothers, when we were torn away from you for a short time (in person, not in thought)'[2] or 'in face, not in heart'. That is, while we may not have the opportunity to see some friends for years on end, yet in heart we are still with them. I find that I have a mental photograph of individuals and their voices, though often it may be as those people were when I last met them – my memory of them is perhaps fifty years out of date, when we were together at school or college. Often when we read their letters, we can almost hear their voices coming through in their written expressions.

Writing to the Philippians, Paul calls Timothy a 'soul brother'[3] a delightful word for a friend. This sense of concern comes through, especially in Paul's second letter to Timothy. It is this human bonding between us which needs to be especially fostered among Christians. Such bonding makes us feel heart concern for them, and thus motivates us to pray. It is so easy to be self-centred and to look at the world only as it affects us personally: we have to learn to start seeing things through the eyes of others. These days there is much talk of 'networking': but sometimes that can be a merely superficial linking of acquaintances, rather than a true bonding with real friends within the Body, the reality evidenced by praying for our friends.

3. Praying is Theological

It's theological – it seems that the Lord is not necessarily limited by our lack of prayer, or the weakness of our expectations, or imagination – for he is 'able to do immeasurably more than all we ask or imagine'.[4] At the same time other scriptures suggest that we can hinder God's work by failing to pray: 'You do not have, because you do not ask God. When you ask, you do not receive because you ask with wrong motives, that you may spend what you get on your pleasures'.[5] If the church is sunk down upon its institutional haunches, like a sleepy, stubborn mule, and cares not whether the unconverted world lives or dies, and prays not for it either: then (to change the metaphor) the visible church is a blocked bottle neck through which grace only feebly trickles.

When we get down on our knees to ask on behalf of others, and there is no selfish motivation, then prayer becomes one of the purest forms of evangelism: we are far away, but we pray to God that he will work. So, as we saw above, we meet repeated injunctions to pray: as a way of our participating in God's mission. Prayer, after all, is not a way of getting my will done in heaven, but a way of getting God's will done on earth. Through prayer, especially when that prayer is enlightened and informed by Scripture, we get in tune with what the Lord wants to happen to people. Lord, what do you want to happen in that missionary's situation, please? We know that it is his will to build his Church.[6] We know that he does not wish anyone to perish but everyone to come to repentance.[7] We know his purpose that there will one day be 'a great multitude that no one could count, from every nation, tribe, people and language' present before the throne and before the Lamb.[8] So we can pray for the planting of churches, the conversion of individuals and outreach into whole nations, peoples and tribes, confident that these have been revealed to us in Scripture as the will of God.

4. Praying Makes Us Actively Involved

This, after all, is what this book is all about: how may Christians become actively involved in God's Mission to all nations? How can we be obedient to Christ's command by sending, rather than being sent? The answer is: by praying. Prayer enables us to participate in Christian work taking place thousands of miles away, in places we have never been to in the past, or will never visit in the future. It used to fascinate me when Billy Graham was holding a special series of evangelistic meetings – say in China or Russia. Thousands of Christian believers who had never been to either country, who spoke not a word of either national language, had their thoughts and prayers directed towards those meetings. For most it was thousands of miles away round the earth's surface: and those prayers were directed to God, who was both present with each one of us as we prayed, and present in the arena where Billy was speaking. The omnipresent God the Father, Son and Spirit is both with us, and with those for whom we are praying: more immediate even than electronic mail.

5. Praying is Pleasing to God

1 Timothy 2:1–3 reads, 'This is good and pleases God our Saviour, who wants all human beings to be saved and come to a knowledge of the truth.' What is 'this' in the context? It is that 'requests, prayers, intercession and thanksgiving be made for all human beings, for kings and those in authority, that we may live peaceful and quiet lives in all godliness and holiness.'

The character of God is revealed in these verses as a God who desires (he does not decree it) that all human beings should be saved and come to a knowledge of the truth. That

God desires something does not mean that it is bound to happen, any more than the Israel to whom God stretched out his hands all day long responded, because God desired that they should. His Son also has given his life a ransom for all human beings. The logic of the passage is that we should pray for all human beings, because the longing of God is their salvation, and because Christ died to make the ransom of all human beings a possible result. Thus for us to pray for what God desires is a very proper thing to do. It pleases him, that we should deeply desire what he already desires, and care enough to pray to him for their salvation.

6. Praying is Commanded by Jesus

The ancestor of Jesus, Boaz of Bethlehem was a 'chief harvester', responsible for getting labourers together to bring in the harvest. Jesus takes up this picture and urges his disciples to 'pray to the Chief Harvester to send out labourers into his harvest field'. It seems in the context both of Matthew 9:38 and Luke 10:2 where this famous expression is used, that having told them to pray to the Chief Harvester to send labourers, the people who are commanded to pray are then themselves sent out by Jesus himself. In Matthew 'Ask the Chief Harvester therefore to send out workers' is followed (10:5) by the observation 'These twelve Jesus sent out'. In Luke the juxtaposition is even closer: 'Ask the Chief Harvester therefore to send out workers into his harvest field. Go! I am sending you.' In both cases it is clear that Jesus is the One who does the sending. He himself is Chief Harvester.

Not only so, but though the contexts are different, in both cases the disciples told to pray are those who also answer the call to go. In Matthew (10:5) it is the Twelve who are commanded to pray, who are then sent out by Jesus. In Luke it is the Seventy Two who are commanded to pray (v.2) who are then (v.3) sent out like lambs among wolves. It is those who care about the masses, and long for them to be saved, who are motivated to pray. In both these passages it looks as though those who care enough to pray, are those whom Jesus sends forth.

7. Praying for what is Relevant

If we look back to the chapter (Chapter VI) describing the different stages of experience, we can see what to pray for people, even if they themselves do not include a specific request along those lines. For the first term missionary, then, prayer for persistence in study, encouragement in developing fluency and courage to use what we have learned is a huge need. But at this stage, when new recruits are junior missionaries living with or under the supervision of more senior missionaries, there is the possibility of personality clashes, often out of frustration with this temporary sense of being useless. Young missionary couples are often so busy with language study, caring for young children, and beginning work in a new language situation, that it is very common for Christian husbands and wives to neglect each other 'for the sake of the work', assuming that because they are Christians they will automatically be rescued from danger. If the husband is travelling a great deal, there will be some tension if the wife feels the burden of having to run the home singlehanded, and that her partner should not be away so much. As the years go by, anxiety for the children, especially when they have to go away from home for primary or secondary education, can create a great deal of stress for the parents.

As we have seen, periods spent back in their home country are certainly not stress free, and people need our friendship and our prayers. At each stage, we need to use our imaginations either, if we are older, remembering what we felt like at the same age, or if we are in the same age group or younger, comparing them with people of the same age whom we know. Just as Dr Spock used to tell parents what their children might be expected to be doing at various ages (and such predictions were normally correct), so we can imagine the particular, unspoken problems of workers in that age group.

8. Praying Works

In our home church we knew Ken, an elderly man who had been seriously ill and was no longer able to work. But he prayed. Someone once arrived at Ken's house and searching for him, finally discovered him planting out some tomato plants in the garden. It proved impossible to attract his attention until quite close. 'You seemed far away,' said the visitor cheerfully. 'Where were you?' and received the reply: 'About five hundred miles east of Moscow!' He had heard of a prayer need and was praying. At times he seemed eccentric : especially his habit of writing down prayer needs on odd bits of paper, so that they fell out of his pocket when he pulled out his handkerchief, reminding him to pray for them.

Ken was once told that a hospital in Africa badly needed an electricity generator. It would cost a great deal of money. Who would have so much to give, Ken wondered. A rich American, perhaps. So Ken started praying that a rich American might give the money for a generator. A week later, there was a ring at the front door bell from someone who had seen a 'Room to Let' notice. 'Say' said the stranger, 'would you have an apartment that I could hire?'.

Ken picked up his visitor's accent: 'Are you an American?' he asked.

'Sure, how did you guess?' replied the stranger. Ken

paused, plucked up courage, and asked more hesitantly: 'Are you . . . a rich American?'

The stranger laughed, said he wasn't particularly rich, but asked what lay behind that question: for he did know some rich Americans. So the hospital in Africa now has a generator – and all because an elderly person took time to find out what was needed and to pray that the need would be met. Life was anything but dull for Ken, never a dull moment.

If Ken asked you whether you had any special prayer requests, you did not hesitate to tell him because Ken's prayers got answered. He commented that he had friends all over the world, including many he had never met. But though prevented by his age and illness from travelling, his friends came to him. When the lives of many are curtailed and limited to television and pottering around the garden, Ken's life was full of interest, as he learned of what was happening in various parts of God's Church, and got into the action through his prayers.

9. Prayer is Warfare

The armour of God (Ephesians 6) was not literal even in the first century, of course. The battle against hostile spiritual forces was in fact carried out through prayer. Many books have been written about such spiritual warfare, and some seem to go over the top in inventing a new speculative mythology of their own. But that should not make us throw out sound biblical teaching with the speculative bathwater when it comes to fighting against spiritual forces of wickedness through prayer. Missionaries have always known that they were up against a powerful and subtle spiritual foe, because that is the teaching of Jesus and the apostles.

'There is constant warfare to be waged against the powers of darkness . . . It is fashionable in the Western world to relegate belief in demons and devils to the realm of mythology, and when mentioned at all it is a matter of jest. But it is no jest in West Africa or any other mission field for that matter' (Rowland Bingham).[9]

One of the classic accounts of such warfare is found in the experience of J O Fraser as he battled for a breakthrough with the Lisu tribe in China, who lived their lives in animistic fear and attempts to placate the evil spirits. Fraser himself is praying, but again and again he writes to his 'prayer circle', ie 'his praying friends'.[10]

> It was fear that kept his Lisu neighbours in bondage, fear which he knew was not unfounded. He was learning that only in a close walk with God and a life of prayer could the powers of darkness be overcome, either in himself or around him. It did seem as if some specially sinister power of evil held sway in Tantsah and the neighbourhood. In his loneliness, Fraser was often conscious of the opposition of unseen foes and fell back with increasing thankfulness upon the prayer-co-operation of his small but growing circle at home.[11]

Two things come through so clearly: his recognition of human weakness and the difficulty of getting down to pray, and his dependence on others far away to join him in the prayer battle:

> Fraser realised his dependence not only upon the Divine Leader, but upon the support of fellow-believers, one with him in Christ. He might be the hand reaching out into the darkness, but not a hand cut off and thrown ahead of the body. (So he writes to his mother) I know you will never fail me in the matter of intercession, but will you think and pray about getting a group of like minded friends, whether few or many, whether in one place or scattered, to join in the same petitions? If you could form a small prayer circle I would write regularly to the members.[12]

This book is concerned with how every believer might play a part in the commission to the whole church to take the whole gospel to the whole world: the role of being a 'sender' is not restricted to sending others to the forefront of the battle. It is a call to all of us to participate in the spiritual battle through our praying. It is not a matter of finding worthy persons to go as substitutes instead of us, but of our joining in the spiritual battle through our prayers, alongside those whom we have sent.

Notes

1 Acts 4:29 and 31
2 1 Thessalonians 2:17
3 Philippians 2:20 (Gk. *isopsuchos*: iso- as in *iso*bar and -*psuchos* as in psychology). See discussion in Chapter IV on friendship.
4 Ephesians 3:20
5 James 4:2–3
6 Matthew 16:18
7 2 Peter 3:9
8 Revelation 7:9
9 Ruth Tucker, *From Jerusalem to Irian Jaya*, (Grand Rapids: Zondervan 1983) p.297
10 Mrs Howard Taylor, *Behind the Ranges: Fraser of Lisuland S.W. China*, (London: Lutterworth Press and CIM, 1944) especially Chap. XII 'The Prayer of Faith'. See also Mrs J O Fraser, *Fraser and Prayer*, (London: China Inland Mission, 1963)
11 *ibid* p.106
12 *ibid* p.85

CHAPTER VIII

A FRESH LOOK AT SELF-SUPPORTING MISSIONARIES

In recent months I have found myself in some developing Third World countries, like Peru and Papua New Guinea, quoting the example of the Moravian congregation in Herrnhut which sent out eight new missionaries every year.[1] Rather naturally people there wanted to know how on earth congregations like theirs with limited resources might hope to follow the Moravians example? Even congregations that have already sent out and are supporting several missionaries recognise that there are limits to the number of missionaries they can afford to support. In Papua New Guinea they can look back to their own history: for they were evangelised first by Christians from the islands of Polynesia, who came westwards in deep sea canoes.[2] They had been subsistence farmers at home, and in Papua they obtained some land and supported themselves from it.

So what of the Moravians? They, too, supported themselves. Being supported by a sending church far away was virtually impossible until the availability of some international banking system. The facts then are these:

In 1732 the first two Moravian brethren were sent out: 'on

foot for Copenhagen, bundles on their backs, thirty shillings in their pockets, and the invincible all-embracing love of Christ in their hearts . . . the modern world wide missionary movement was born.'[3]

When Dr Regnier wished to go out to Surinam, the only country in Latin America sympathetic to Protestants at that time, as a medical missionary, he was interrogated by Count Zinzendorf like this:

Z: What do you intend to do in Surinam?
R: I will do my best to earn my living and to bring sinners to Christ.
Z: How do you intend to get there?
R: I shall simply trust Christ to show me the way.
Z: How long do you intend to stay there?
R: I shall stay there either till I die or till the elders call me to another field.[4]

To understand this approach to sending out missionaries who must be entirely self-supporting we have to understand what lay behind these principles of operation. This way of working was not only a matter of necessity, but a means of example to others:

The missionary must teach the heathen the dignity of labour by fending for himself and earning his own living. In the days of Zinzendorf, the missionary received from the church just sufficient money to take him to the port of departure. Often the missionary walked to the port and then worked his passage across the ocean. On the mission field he took up whatever occupation would provide him with the bare amount of food and clothing. On 30 March 1756, Solomon Schumann wrote from Surinam: 'Brother Kamm is picking coffee; Brother Wenzel is mending shoes; Brother Schmidt is making a dress for a customer; Brother Doerfer is digging the garden; Brother Brambly is working on the canal.'[5]

In view of its subject therefore this chapter must be rather different from the largely methodological sections of the book so far. Much of this chapter is a Bible study on Paul's method of support. This is important, because we need to work and pray for a substantial shift in the way churches think about missions.

Let me try to shock you by suggesting that Paul was 'a layman'. The early church did not accept the modern distinction between Christians who differed in the spiritual gifts with which God had sovereignly endowed them: they were all equally members of the people of God.[6] I make this point because we are guilty of an anachronism if we think of Paul, as most of us have been doing, as 'a full-time Christian worker' of the kind we have today. We think of Paul as the model missionary: and so he is, but not the model of a church-supported missionary. The model Paul provides is that of a self-supporting or bi-vocational missionary! As we shall see, Paul could argue that while all Christian workers had the right to be supported because of their labours, as a matter of principle he (and Barnabas) refused to make use of that right. He quite deliberately chose to work for his own support. This in no way detracts from his extraordinary achievement: but rather enhances it.

1. Early Examples of Self-supporting Missionaries (Bi-vocationals)

Of necessity the majority of missionaries for the first seventeen centuries of church history were self-supporting. The possibility of being supported on a regular basis by a church in a sending country is a relative novelty of the past two hundred years, only made possible by the availability of international banks. Hudson Taylor was one of the very first customers of the Hongkong and Shanghai Bank. When the Antioch church collected money for the relief of Christians in Palestine, it had to be physically carried there by Barnabas and Saul.[7] It is only because the last two centuries almost entirely coincide with the era of Protestant missions that we have tended to assume this is the usual and normal way for missionaries to be supported. As we shall see most of the earlier Roman Catholic missionaries and many of the earlier Protestant missionaries were in fact self-supporting. (See Benjamin Broomhall's summary of how CIM missionaries were being supported in 1895 p.29).

Many celibate Roman Catholic missionaries who took the Christian message to the world[8] long before protestant missions had even started were self-supporting. Mateo Ricci, a Jesuit in Peking supported himself by making and repairing clocks (for which he was paid a stipend by the Emperor of China), and by using his skills as a cartographer to make and sell maps.

Last year my wife and I made a pilgrimage to the grave of Robert Morrison in Macao: the first Protestant missionary to get into China. Arriving in Canton from Scotland in 1807, he supported himself by working as an interpreter for the East India Company. William Carey first supported himself as manager of an indigo plantation, and later by teaching at the Calcutta college. The wife of his colleague, Sarah Marshman, also brought in money to support 'the Serampore Trio' by running a small school. Indeed at a time when the newly formed missionary societies were reluctant to employ single women, a number of them 'went overseas unsupported by any society and worked for long periods, as missionaries in every sense but the technical one'.[9] Among those who opened fee-paying schools were Miss Whately, daughter of the Archbishop of Dublin, and Mary Ann

Aldersley. She had some private means, and started an Indo-Chinese School in Java and in 1842 opened a school in Ningpo, China where she was assisted by daughters of various missionaries including Maria Dyer, the future Mrs. Hudson Taylor.

When we discuss fresh possibilities of self-supporting missionaries today we need to remember that in previous generations the majority of missionaries had to be bi-vocational in order to support themselves.

2. The Example of the Apostle Paul and his Associates

If you study Paul's letters afresh you begin to realise that he was actually a bi-vocational missionary. Luke in Acts only actually mentions Paul working as a tentmaker in Corinth and Ephesus.[10] But Paul himself widens our understanding.

In 1 Corinthians 9:5,6 Paul speaks of 'the other apostles, the Lord's brothers and Cephas (Peter)' on the one hand as a mono-vocational group, and there names himself and Barnabas as the only ones 'who must work for a living', and are thus bi-vocational. There are two very obvious reasons for this distinction.

(i) First, while Paul had a highly portable trade, requiring only an awl and a few needles, easily carried in his pack, Peter and his fishing partners[11] could scarcely drag their fishing boats, laden with nets, along with them on the Roman roads!

(ii) Secondly, the Twelve and the Seventy two had been commanded by Jesus to take nothing for their journey and on entering a house to 'stay there, eating and drinking whatever they give you, for the worker deserves his wages'.[12] It may well be that this was culturally acceptable within the Jewish culture, and it is perhaps significant that there are no examples of Jewish rabbis combining teaching Torah with trade until the second century after the fall of Jerusalem and the Jewish wars. Certainly we know that it had been agreed that Paul and Barnabas would go to the Gentiles, while the Jerusalem apostles went to the Jews.[13] By contrast, Paul seems to have made something of a habit of antagonising Jewish communities in whose synagogues he preached Christ.[14]

These would seem two significant factors in understanding why some of the apostles could claim their right to be supported, while others chose not to use their right, but chose to work for their living, and thus to be self-supporting bi-vocationals. To this list we may add the names of Luke (for medicine is also a highly portable trade) and Aquila and Priscilla, with whom Paul worked in Corinth. Aquila and Prisca then accompanied Paul to Ephesus, where he left them, and where they were later able to explain the way of God more accurately to the eloquent Apollos. They may well have been the first church planters in Ephesus. When Paul returned, as he had promised to do, we may presume he joined them again in their workshop.[15]

3. How Extensive was Paul's Practice of Self-support?

Paul asserts that self-support was for him a general principle.[16] It is also clear that at times he was prepared to accept support from churches, other than the one in which he was actually working at the time.[17] What evidence is there of his working more regularly?

First Missionary Journey. As we have already seen, Paul tells us that Barnabas also worked to support himself, though we do not know how he did this or what his craft skills were. This suggests that even on the first excursion to Cyprus and up into Galatia both of them were self-supporting.

Second Missionary Journey. Paul insists that he worked 'night and day' in Thessalonica[18] and confirms Luke's account regarding Corinth 'we grow weary from the work of our own hands'.[19] This then covers a substantial part of the second journey.

Third Missionary Journey. Paul confirms that he was working in Ephesus 'to this present hour' and carries this forward to his anticipated return visit to Corinth.[20]

Roman Imprisonment under House Arrest. When under house arrest in Rome the words 'at his own expense' suggest that Paul may have continued to work there also.[21]

4. Possible Models for Paul's Practice

The Greeks generally despised manual labour; Plato said that no artisan could ever become a citizen of the state, while Aristotle said that nobody could become a citizen until he had dropped his trade for ten years. This helps us understand Paul's frequent statements about being despised, and looked down on. Over and above that, tanning animal skins was a despised trade in Jerusalem,[22] and this distaste may have extended to working with the skins of the black Cilician goats used in tent making. Trades involving dead animals are still widely despised in Asia because of Buddhism. However there is a well preserved tanner's workshop in Masada.

As explained above there are no first century examples of Jewish rabbis exercising a trade, so that the most likely model in the Graeco-Roman world is that of wandering philosophers. Philosophers in those days might be supported in four different ways:

(1) By charging tuition or lecture fees, like college lecturers today. Socrates stoutly refused to do this.
(2) By attaching themselves to wealthy households as residential tutors and intellectuals, as Aristotle and Plato did, rather like tutors and governesses formerly in

English stately homes. Aristotle had been a tutor in Assos, where Paul re-boarded his ship after walking from Troas.

(3) By begging, as many Cynic philosophers did, like Diogenes of Sinope. Cynics were so-called not because they were 'cynical' in our sense, but from the Greek word for 'dog' because they lived dog-like, free foragers, who slept in public parks, washed in public baths, roamed where they pleased and begged and scavenged what they could (like a London squatter, but in a much warmer and more sympathetic climate). Paul is actually borrowing their language when he calls himself 'free' and claims to be 'self-sufficient'.[23]

(4) Some philosophers supported themselves by working with their hands as Paul did. Simon the shoemaker conversed with Socrates in his workshop.[24] Hock argues that the workshops of shoemakers and leather workers were 'a conventional social setting for intellectual discourse'.[25] Xenophon actually describes Socrates accompanied by some of his students discussing philosophy both in the marketplace and in various workshops, including that of a saddler. Some Cynic philosophers travelled even more extensively than Paul, like the man appropriately known as Peregrinus.

5. Who Needed the Tents Made by Aquila, Priscilla and Paul Anyway?

Some people have argued with some justification, that 'tentmaker'[26] is an inappropriate word to describe bi-vocational workers today, because Paul was first and foremost a professional preacher and evangelist, and only made tents when he had to because he was out of cash! My friend Peter Pattisson (himself an extremely effective bi-vocational missionary in

Korea researching into and treating tuberculosis of the hip and spine while at the same time engaging in a great deal of evangelistic and pastoral work) wrote an article in which he said:

> The widespread use of the term [tent maker] gives a pseudo-biblical authority to a minor biblical allusion. Paul does not seem to have engaged in tent making because the Corinthians were in need of tents. The terminology of tent making too easily undervalues the place of professional service, and nurtures the all too prevalent 'means to an end' mentality whereby young people see a job simply as a door to the 'real job' of evangelism.[27]

I agree with Peter about the wrong-mindedness of the 'means to an end' mentality. A proper biblical doctrine of work means that all Christians are to perform their daily work and exercise their professions to the glory of God (as well as to satisfy their employers and colleagues). But what makes us say that Paul was not committed to tent making in the way that Christian teachers, doctors or businessmen are committed to their professions working abroad today? I think we have misunderstood and undervalued the role that tent making played in Paul's life and ministry.

The ancients presumably did not need tents for young people wanting to hike and camp in the mountains. So what did they use them for?

(1) Tents were used by Roman armies in the field. It has even been suggested that Paul's father may have been granted citizenship for making tents for the Roman army, and taught his son the same trade.

(2) Tents were used by the crews and passengers of ships, who could not see to navigate at night, and as they stayed in sight of land while they could, would also

put ashore when it got dark. See for example Luke's description of the journey from Miletus to Cos, Rhodes and Patara, and subsequently from, Tyre to Ptolemais and on to Caesarea.[28] Streams of ships passed through the two ports of Corinth, on both the Adriatic and Aegean sides of the isthmus, indeed many were manhandled across the *diolkos* tramway on rollers. Corinth was a great place for selling tents to them.

(3) Tents were in great demand for spectators to the Isthmian Games held in Corinth every two years.

You will see that a firm of tent makers in Corinth was exceedingly well-placed to supply this not inconsiderable market, and that Aquila and Priscilla had a shrewd eye to business!

Most apprentice contracts specify working from sunrise to sunset, so that 'night and day' suggests Paul started work before sunrise and continued until sunset, and did this for six days every week from Sunday to Friday, taking the sabbath off to go to the synagogue for as long as they could take him. However his working day would be reduced by a very long lunch break in the middle. If you have ever tried to shop during a summer afternoon in Greece, you will have discovered that shops are closed for a long siesta between 1–5 pm and then re-open. We do know that in Ephesus Paul discoursed daily in the lecture hall of Tyrannus, and according to the Western text from 11 am to 4 pm – the hottest and sleepiest time of the day.

6. What was Paul's Workshop like?

Murphy O'Connor[29] has an interesting section on workshops excavated in Corinth. The shops in the North Market at Corinth were four metres high, just under four metres deep and varied in width from 2.8 – 4 metres. The doorway was the only source of light, like the open shop fronts still so typical in Asia. This means that only a few people could get right inside the shop at any one time, but such shops are designed to spread out across the sidewalk. Apart from Paul, Aquila and Priscilla there would be space for only a few customers, together with seekers after truth who had heard Paul in the synagogue, and now wanted opportunity for more personal conversation. Imagine Paul punching holes with his awl and stitching with his needle, perhaps waving them in the air to emphasise a particular point. 'Working, we proclaimed' gives a charming picture, of combining work with preaching. As Murphy O'Connor puts it:

> One of the advantages of leather working was that he could easily do both; the environment was clean and pleasant, and the only sound the soft thump as the awl went in. In slack periods he could stand in the door and buttonhole those whom he thought might listen . . . it is difficult to imagine that his dynamic personality and utter conviction did not quickly make him a 'character' of the neighbourhood, and this would have drawn the curious, not merely the idlers but also those genuinely seeking.[30]

Paul tells us he had a far from easy life: he speaks of 'exhausting toil';[31] being hungry and thirsty, weary from the work of our own hands;[32] in toil and hardship; cold and naked.[33] Paul working at the manual labour the Greek gentry despised, gives us a fresh perspective on many scriptures. In the eyes of many, such work was 'slavish' and certainly not to be expected of a Roman citizen. 'You are held in honour: we in disrepute.'[34] 'Though I am free with respect to all, I have made myself a slave to all'.[35] 'Did I commit a sin by humbling myself . . . because I proclaimed God's good news to you free of charge?'[36] We should not see him as moving only among an urban elite, for even when he did benefit from such hospitality, he must return to his daily toil, except at such times as generous gifts arrived from such as the Philippian church.

Summing up then: it is clear that for Paul making tents was not a casual sideline to be picked up occasionally when church life was slow or evangelism was 'out of season': but for six days a week. Hard work from dawn to dusk was his daily lot, and that as a matter of principle and example to others. When in prison, he evangelised Praetorian guard and fellow prisoners, like Onesimus, alike. This is consistent with a man who evangelised in the course of his daily working life. The mechanical nature of his manual labour made it possible to talk, teach, admonish, counsel and evangelise at the same time.

The snag today is that not many contemporary 'tent makers' have work which is so intellectually undemanding that it permits conversational evangelism while exercising professional responsibilities. Indeed to preach on the course of one's daily work might in some circles be regarded as most unprofessional: though it might be profitably discussed where this notion comes from, and whether it is really a Christian notion. Why should a surgeon not pray for skill and help in God's providence, if he is a believing surgeon? Muslims have less embarrassment in praying than most of us. And should teachers not pray for God's help in being good teachers?

7. Self-support in Today's World

Now how are we to apply all this? Generally, we may say that for Christian workers to be self-supporting is just as biblical as for them to be supported entirely by churches: neither method of support is less biblical or more spiritual than the other. The fact that Paul and Barnabas supported themselves, while other apostles did not is clear.[37] The fact that rural traditions are different from urban situations, or that ministry within Jewish culture may be different from that in Gentile culture gives to us today a flexibility to vary support with what is appropriate. No missionary candidate should assume that being 'church-supported' is necessarily the only proper or right way for them. The self-supporting option should be seriously considered, especially by those with technical skills to offer.

In our introductory section I illustrated from a recent visit, how many Christians from many nationalities are working in one country, not as church-supported professionals, but as self-supported people in a wide variety of roles. The Chief Harvester has his own methods of 'creative access' in stationing his men and women in the places where he wants them. For all of them Paul the tent maker is a compelling model and inspiration.

If Paul is our model of preaching in the course of a busy working life, we must see secular professional work as a credible spiritual option: it has the clearest of biblical mandates. The challenge is still a missionary challenge involving sacrifice of income and comfort: to be self-supporting one must work hard at one's profession all day, and at evangelism and church planting in all one's spare time. Self-supporting, 'Tent Makers' are not a whit inferior to church-supported missionaries: they are not a second best. They need to be just as spiritual, at least as gifted, and they need at least as much prayer from supporting churches, if not more! It's just that they don't need money from the church. If this is the Chief Harvester's will for your life, it will be a rewarding one. So pray to the Chief Harvester and discover what he wants you to do with your life. It is significant that the Lord commanded both the Twelve and the Seventy to pray to the Chief Harvester, and then sent all of them out in his service. Pray to him that he will determine both where he wants you to be sent and what he wants you to do there.

I have recently been invited to speak to students in Papua New Guinea and have been much intrigued that almost every meeting is to centre on Mission: presumably with a view to New Guineans themselves becoming missionaries to less evangelised parts of the world. For developing countries with a relatively low per capita income, the idea of being self-supporting missionaries is a realistic one for they do not have wealthy churches able to support many of their members. A return to the earlier, traditional methods of self-support may be the best way ahead.

8. A Shift in our Thinking

There are two main reasons why we need such a shift in our thinking about missions.

(1) The first is well expressed in Christy Wilson's' book written in 1979, when he quotes Philip Butler of InterCristo:

> When was the last time you heard from your pulpit on Sunday morning 'Let's pray for Charlie Jones, our missionary with Shell Oil in Caracas'? The idea that a person can function in the commercial, military or government arena overseas as a missionary is largely overlooked if not discredited in our churches. This myopic view of Christian service has seriously stunted the Church's growth worldwide. It has blinded us in our ability to mount an effective Great Commission campaign under the headship of our Lord Jesus Christ. Local churches should view these self-supporting individuals as real missionaries – worthy of all the prayer and other benefits flowing from the local fellowship.[38]

If we were more familiar with the history of Protestant missions we would know of the huge influence of Christian soldiers and government officials in India, who saw the need and the opportunity and pleaded with missionary societies to send workers, and often made it possible from their own pockets. We have already mentioned Valpy French as a linguist (p.93). But much of his work was first conceived by Christian laymen, and funded by them. It was the Lieutenant Governor of the North West Provinces James Thomason (son of one of Simeon's famous five chaplains) who urged the CMS to open a college in Agra, which Valpy French did in 1853. And the evangelistic Derajat mission which French opened along the North West Frontier was funded by a gift of a thousand pounds from the Commissioner for the region, Colonel Reynall Taylor, said to be the best swordsman in India.[39]

At the very end of his life when as a retired bishop Valpy French visited Jeddah, the port of Mecca, with the young American missionary Samuel Zwemer, he mentions how three years earlier General Haig had entered the town with a bag of Bibles which were all confiscated.[40] When Mackay of Uganda is urging a mission to Arabia, he writes: 'It is the deliberate conviction of General Haig that in Oman, the capital of which is Muscat "there are important openings for the Gospel."' The same General Haig wrote in the *Church Mission Intelligencer*, July 1887 an article on 'Arabia as a Mission Field'.[41]

(2) Once Christians become accustomed to praying for members of their churches who are supporting themselves through employment overseas, they will realise afresh the obligation upon them as Christians employed in secular business at home to work for the Lord through their everyday employment. This could have a significant impact upon the witness of Christians at home. Thus the 'senders' would

realise that the only difference between them and the 'sent' overseas is geographical location: after all, 'overseas' is a mere accident of continental drift. All of us are equally involved in the whole church's mission to the whole world, and should be equally committed to our Master's cause to bring the gospel to all human beings of every nation.

Notes

1 See Chapter II
2 See John M Hitchen, 'Our South Pacific Missionary Heritage – The Forgotten Central Strand' article in *Transformation*
3 A J Lewis, *Zinzendorf the Ecumenical Pioneer* (London: S C M Press, 1962) p.279
4 *ibid* p.90
5 *ibid* p.92
6 The word 'lay' is often used to describe non-clerical persons, and derives from the Greek word *laos* which refers to the people of God as a whole: in other words a born-again clergyman is also a 'lay person'!
7 Acts 11:30; 12:25
8 If the more Protestant among us have question marks about this in view of some of the syncretistic approaches adopted by some of them, that embarrassment would be shared by many Roman Catholics as well. That they as well as many Protestants exported forms of cultural Christianity cannot be denied.
9 Jocelyn Murray, *Anglican and Protestant Missionary Societies in Great Britain: their use of women as missionaries from the late 18th to the late 19th Century* (*Femmes en Mission*, August 1990).
10 Acts 18:1–3; l 20:33–35
11 Luke 5:7,10

12 Luke 9:3; 10:7

13 Galatians 2:9

14 Acts 13:45, 46, 50; 14:2, 5, 19

15 Acts 18:18–19, 26

16 1 Corinthians 9:15–18; Acts 20:34–35

17 2 Corinthians 11:7–9; l, Phil 4:14–19

18 1 Thessalonians 2:9

19 1 Corinthians 4:12

20 1 Corinthians 4:11, 12; 2 Corinthians 12:14, 15, 16

21 Acts 28:30

22 Joachim Jeremias, *Jerusalem in the Time of Jesus*, (London: S C M Press, 1969) p.308

23 1 Corinthians 9:1; Philippians 4:10

24 Plutarch, *Maxime cum. Princ. phil. diss.* 776B

25 Hock, *The Social Context of Paul's Ministry: Tentmaking and Apostleship* (Philadelphia: Fortress Press, 1982 and Edinburgh: T & T Clark) p.31

26 See J Christy Wilson's excellent book *Today's Tentmakers* (Wheaton: Tyndale House Publishers, 1979) and see also T Yamamori, *God's New Envoys* (Portland, Multnomah Press 1987)

27 Peter Pattisson, *The Trouble with Tentmakers* (East Asia Millions, Feb-Mar 1987) pp.28–29

28 Acts 21:1–8

29 Jerome Murphy O'Connor, *St Paul's Corinth: Texts and Archeology* (Minnesota: Liturgical Press, 1983) p. 175–178

30 O'Connor *ibid* p.169

31 1 Thessalonians 2:9

32 1 Corinthians 4:11,12

33 2 Corinthians 11:27

34 1 Corinthians 4:11

35 1 Corinthians 9:19

36 2 Corinthians 11:7

37 1 Corinthians 9:3–6
38 Christy Wilson, *ibid* p.143
39 Herbert Birks, *Life of T Valpy French: Bishop of Lahore* (London: John Murray 1895) Vol 1 p.125
40 *ibid* Vol 2 p.350
41 JW Mackay, *Mackay of Uganda*, (London: Hodder & Stoughton,1898) p.419,426

CHAPTER IX

MOBILISING EVERY CHURCH MEMBER – THE ROLE OF THE CHURCH MISSION COMMITTEE

This chapter might seem a dreary account of how to organise a committee. However I hope it won't be dreary and that it will be useful. Perhaps the first thing to do is to know what the church leaders are asking of you, and define some terms of reference.

The Evangelical Missionary Alliance and the Evangelical Alliance have produced an excellent folder entitled 'Your Local Church and World Mission: How to bring world mission into focus in the local church'. It consists of a number of worksheets: How to Start a World Mission Programme in your church; How to Form a World Mission Action Group etc. I warmly recommend this: it can be obtained by writing to The Evangelical Missionary Alliance, Whitefield House, 186 Kennington Park Road, LONDON SE11 4BR.

1. Starting from Scratch

Some years ago I spent from 8 am to 6 pm with more than a hundred young Indonesian graduates all thinking of missionary service. Though they belonged to the largest Christian church in Asia (proportionally to the population: the Korean and Singaporean churches would be much larger), they all had one thing in common: none of their churches had ever yet sent out a missionary! They were the guinea pigs on whom their churches must experiment and learn by making mistakes, so we decided to start praying for seven model sending churches. Few readers will be in quite such a scratch situation as that, but even today some of us might belong to a local congregation without any recognised structure for sending people out. Some who want to serve others feel that if there is such a lack of interest, their only solution is to leave such a church and join a different one! That course of action will do nothing to help your fellow church members become involved in our Lord's Mission to the World.

1. Scratch and Pray!

That first step the Indonesian Christians took, of starting to pray about their local church in a missionary sending context, is one that we can all take. We can start praying to be led to likeminded people already in our church, and also pray that newcomers with a similar concern might move into the area and join the church. So we start from scratch, by praying and scratching around to find other people to pray with us. When two or three start meeting to pray, even once a month, for things to happen, then you have made a beginning.

At some point you will need to make some kind of approach or proposal to the leaders of your congregation: and that is one of the things you will want to pray about when you meet. Perhaps inviting a visiting speaker to talk about missions might be a first step. Then in discussing issues raised by the preacher afterwards, while the iron is hot, you may have a good opportunity for raising the issue of a church policy and programme. As our earlier chapter on the role of pastors in missions has shown, it will be difficult to proceed without the support of the leadership. That support will lie on a spectrum from informed enthusiasm and encouragement at one end, to a not so enthusiastic agreement to allow you to try your hand at the other: hopefully downright refusal is not an option. Praying for God to move the hearts of human leaders has to be our first step. There can be few churches that really have to start completely from scratch, as links with individuals or denominational missionary societies can all provide some kind of stepping stones to something more wholehearted and better organised.

Several things are against us here. Some of us have an inbuilt disdain for organisation and methodology, and tend to feel that happy go lucky improvisation and serendipitous chaos is somehow more spiritual. (This may be more closely linked with inborn laziness, reluctance to stick our necks out and our refusal to take on any more responsibilities, than we want to recognise.) Other people by temperament like to have everything spelled out on paper, and the transatlantic tendency is very much that way. When I was OMF's General Director, a group of my fellow OMF missionaries once gave me a notebook entitled Mike's Mission Handbook – in which all the pages were blank! So you can understand that temperamentally I am not so enthusiastic for putting everything down on paper! But I recognise that many of my fellow Christians like it that way, and there is no doubt that it does help people starting from scratch to spell things out. Once everything has been organised, we need to bring in more flexibility and to recognise that human suggestions on paper are not laws of the Medes and Persians that cannot be broken. And if we have prayed over the whole matter together first, and prayed for simplicity and decency and order, and have consulted with God's Holy Spirit at every stage, we may trust for something simple, straightfoward, clear and lucid.

2. Start Small, and Inform the Church in Digestible Bites

Grandiose schemes will frighten everybody and panic the church treasurer! Start with just one or two projects. Better still, start by supporting someone respected by the congregation as a whole, and whose work catches the enthusiasm of all. 'A Plan to Reach the Whole World in This Generation' may sound impressive, but strains the credulity of even the most enthusiastic of us. Much better would be: 'How to assist John and Mary Smith, whom we know and love, reach one neglected people group like the Kurds, Mongolians or Uzbeks.' Something personalised and focused is a much more immediate and realisable goal within the grasp of any congregation.

Communists used to talk of politicising the masses, that is, making ordinary people politically aware and determined to get action for change. Our Christian task is to educate the congregation, making them aware of world need, and making them want to do something practical about it in addition to giving money (which can be a cop out!). It can be a gradual process of helping people to learn by doing. The committee learns about the problems of missionaries (as outlined in Chapter VI) as they go along. The congregation also learns as it prays about the missionaries they care about. A simple statement which sets out the committee's function in a user-friendly way can be very helpful. You want the congregation to feel they have a handle on what you're doing.

3. Get People Together for Action and Prayer

If people are going to form a working party to help a single missionary or family pack up their home, or to organise a valedictory meeting, or a send off, or prepare some accommodation, and stock the larder for somebody coming home, all of these provide natural occasions for people to pray together. In this way the natural connection between caring for people and praying for them develops. It may be best to avoid calling it a 'Prayer Meeting' to avoid confusion with existing gatherings, so call it the Smiths' Supporters Club, Jones Sending Society, Friends of Turkey or whatever. Some hard work needs to be done to keep devising interesting presentations – letters, slides, telephone calls, E-mail, faxes, videos so that the group feel really in touch with the up-to-the-minute triumphs and trials of the one they are supporting. The recipe of not too often and not too long, helps motivate people to give such a group priority. Try to avoid making it one more meeting where half the time is taken up doing the same unspecific things as any other meeting (we do not have to sing, unless it's relevant!). Rather than having people looking at their watches, they should leave looking forward to the next meeting!

4. Produce a Short Statement of Mission Policy

The danger here is to produce something so comprehensive, embracing every possible combination of circumstances, that hardly anybody has time to read it all and still less to grasp the overall scheme. Half a side of A4 approved by the leadership and understood by the congregation may be all that is needed to start with. Certain basic questions need to be answered:

(1) With whom should members of the congregation discuss their calling, suitability and training? Should it be church leaders, or if they are too busy and wish to delegate it, other experienced Christians forming

some kind of church mission committee? Who decides on calling and suitability?

(2) Who is authorised to advise over suitable training, and decide whether or not to propose that the church give some financial help?

(3) How will people be approved and selected either as church supported workers, or recognised self-supporting missionaries? What is the mechanism and procedure of screening, selection and appointment? Who recommends budget allocations? Long term financial planning must come in here.

(4) How, in the short term, are the workers to be sent on their way, and then, in the long haul, to be kept in touch with and prayed for?

(5) How is the Missionary Committee selected, how long do they serve, to whom are they accountable, and how often must they report back to the church?

(6) How will the congregation as a whole be enabled to take ownership of this programme, so that it is not seen as a sideshow run by enthusiasts, but as a corporate operation in which every Christian feels that they are senders? This is the most important goal, to be kept constantly in mind by any group or sub-committee with delegated responsibility. How can they keep everybody else informed and involved? Some clear procedures of communication so that the leadership and the membership as a whole are kept informed are essential.

5. Avoiding Fossilization

Once policies have been formulated, discussed and decided, the danger is just to file the documents, and forget all about the programme in the general bustle of the church's life.

Putting policies down on paper does not actually achieve very much at all, unless they are vigorously implemented and continually followed up. The policies, and even more the practices, need to be carefully reviewed every year, and reported on, and changes proposed before the annual church meeting.

A church body is a living organism that exists twenty-four hours a day, seven days a week. Just as we as individuals can get out of bed, visit the bathroom, wash and shave, eat breakfast and set out for work, more or less on automatic pilot without needing conscious thought, so even more can congregations go through the regular motions of weekly services and activities without much conscious thought on the part of the bulk of the membership. Only the leaders think much (assuming they do!). We need to keep our 'sending' responsibility constantly in the forefront of people's thinking.

The danger of any church missions committee is that the congregation, once it has delegated to them, will then marginalise them! For any church, 'sending' is as much one of its functions as 'teaching', 'evangelism' and 'worship', so 'sending' needs to find a regular place in the weekly life of the church and to be allocated an appropriate amount of time. This has to be worked at, and the growing enthusiasm and involvement of church leadership is important here. More and more 'worship' is being delegated to 'worship teams' that are a law to themselves. It used to be church organists and choir masters who were a thorn in the side of the leadership. (Question: What's the difference between a terrorist and a church organist? Answer: You can negotiate with a terrorist!) But many such worship teams fail to integrate with the teaching ministry of the church, so that services lack overall cohesion and this is a worrisome trend. We need to ensure that 'sending' is not regarded as a sideshow intruding upon the even tenor of church life, but is thoroughly integrated into the teaching ministry of the church leadership. 'Mission slots' need to be filled in full consultation and harmony with the teaching ministry.

6. The Use of Literature

The written word often fastens in the mind much more thoroughly than the spoken word in these days of reduced concentration span. Thus reading Stott's *Basic Christianity* or Lewis's *Mere Christianity* may serve to inform the mind with an understanding of the Christian gospel, in a way that an evangelistic message focusing on one aspect of the gospel may fail to do. In the same way, well-written books about mission, biographies, and stories of churches and evangelism in other countries, will fill in a lot of the detail that talks or sermons cannot provide in the time available. The spoken word hopefully will motivate people to action and also to study the written word.

Operation World (which is regularly updated) needs to be a standard item of furniture, available in every Christian home. It can be kept on top of the television set, as a constant reminder when any international news item appears, to check up on the position of our brothers and sisters in Christ in that country: whether it be Iraq, Fiji, Ukraine, Nigeria or Kuwait. How many Christians are there? Are they free to evangelise or an oppressed minority? Is the church growing? What denominations are represented? How can we pray for them intelligently? Because any local church must inevitably focus upon certain people and certain countries, this book enables us all to widen our concerns and our understanding of churches around the world. Best of all, it could be kept on our bedside tables or the kitchen table and used as a source of prayer material. It also provides a wealth of information on particular countries about which the church may have a focused interest.

You could give monthly summary digests, country by country, to church members along with other church news and information. If those can be reinforced with maps and diagrams on an overhead projector, and accompanied by prayer for that part of the world, in the course of a church's main weekly gathering, the information will become much easier to grasp.

Operation Mobilisation have long made available world maps, which can be displayed on the kitchen or living room wall, and together with photographs of church missionaries and other friends used as part of family prayers. OM also offer small packets of needy country cards, each carrying the basic demographic information, a map, and major prayer requests. The monthly prayer sheets with a topic for every day issued by many missionary societies are also useful for family prayers, and well-organised churches often produce their own especially to assist their members in praying for their missionaries.

Book reviews, well presented by people who have actually read the book in question all the way through (!), and who can recommend it with genuine enthusiasm because it has helped, stimulated and informed them, also serve as a stimulus to help all church members keep up to date with recent publications and enable them to benefit from well-written material.

CHAPTER X

THE SENDERS AND THE SENT: KEEPING IN TOUCH BOTH WAYS

When the relationship is working properly, it is wonderful. The ones sent can feel profound gratitude for belonging to a body which does not amputate them, or leave them stranded out of sight, out of mind, but keeps in close touch, and shares in their pains and their joys through believing prayer. It is so encouraging to meet the missionary who can enthuse about his home congregation, as a model of missionary enthusiasm and commitment. Equally it is wonderful to meet churches who are thrilled at their participation in work thousands of miles away through their chosen representatives. But it does not always work so well, for there are psychological barriers to be overcome.

Going to work in another country is a curious Alice through the Looking Glass experience, or if you will, it's a bit like travelling through the wardrobe into Narnia. That one's home country still exists is not in doubt, and yet in a way it seems curiously unreal. So many new experiences jam one's mental switchboard within a few short days, one's former life seems to have receded rapidly into the past. This sensation was more marked in the days when weeks at sea, calling at a variety of ports, had also intervened since leaving home. But even after a relatively brief intercontinental flight one still seems to have entered into a different world. The new life is so totally absorbing, that one might as well be on a different planet. To start with, recollections of life at home can be quite vivid, but they steadily fade throughout the early months, especially when people are absorbed in language study. We all know similar experiences when we move from one city to another, or even when we go away on holiday.

This means we have a kind of double jeopardy: most of those in our home church have no knowledge of the country we are now working in, and do not find it easy to visualise us. Two letters stick in my mind: one from an earnest Christian talking about 'the black people in Singapore' (can they really have read our letters at all?) and another from a lovely old lady, who hearing of a tidal wave in Japan, had consulted an atlas (so far so good!) but had then been deeply troubled to discover 'how narrow' the Japanese islands were. Her mental picture seemed to be of us hanging grimly on to some bamboos, while a huge wave umpteen thousand feet high, swept right across the islands of Japan. That may seem laughably extreme, but most of us carry around with us extraordinary caricatures of what other countries are like.

When we arrived in Japan, they thought the English moved around in dense smog wearing top hats and bearskins. At that time the English thought the Japanese ambled along in coloured kimono over red lacquered bridges under the cherry blossom with a background of snow capped volcanoes. Later the image changed to factories and golf! But from the missionary side, and the missionary has after all lived in both worlds, there is also the corresponding difficulty of reconciling these two so different and apparently disassociated worlds. This helps to explain the extraordinary experience of returning to one's homeland after four or five years' absence. I remember vividly being collected at Dover – happy to be home, and with so much that was familiar, but feeling as mystified as a Gulliver in Lilliput or Brobdignag. We arrived in the midst of the sixties miniskirt revolution – and it was quite startling after conservative Japan. I asked my brother-in-law whether one could ever get used to this quite extraordinary public exposure of yards of female thigh. As human beings we do accommodate to our new environment, and often to such an extent that the old familiar environment seems to recede like a distant dream. We know that the familiar world still exists: letters arrive with familiar handwriting and postmarks, but already reality seems to be retreating.

I have given some space to this, because all of us, whether senders or the sent, need to realise that disciplined effort is needed on both sides to try and build bridges between these two 'worlds' from both ends. There is a danger on both sides that it will become a chore – attempted out of duty or necessity, but seen as a tiresome interruption into our 'local' lives. For this reason it may be helpful to give reasons why the effort to 'keep in touch' is important, significant and essential for both parties.

1. Why Senders Need to Keep in Touch with their Missionaries

(1) *The body*. The work is not just their work, but our work. They are still members of our local church body – we have sent them off, but we have not amputated them. They are, if you like, hands of our local church body stretched out across the oceans, in order to function on behalf of the whole congregation. They are our representatives, selected by us, and when they work, pray, preach and witness, our local

church is at work through them. We sent these people out, and they are there because we understood the will of God that they should go. We then are responsible, under God, for their continuing welfare and support. We must therefore do our utmost to understand their situation, to encourage them by every means in our power and to go on steadily praying for them and bringing them before the throne of grace. We cannot responsibly send them out, and then forget them.

(2) *The vine*. Christ is the vine and we are the branches, and so are they and the overseas Christians with whom they live and work. We are all nourished and sustained by Jesus' life flowing through us through his promised Holy Spirit, who indwells us all. There is not only some notional connection still linking us together, but we are all linked through Christ's life holding us together in the One great worldwide vine. We must appreciate their need out there: they can be lonely, discouraged, ill, overworked, and they need us to support them. For us to be heedless, careless and disinterested, while they suffer, is inhuman, let alone unchristian. The New Testament indicates the extent to which Christians are involved in each other's suffering. It goes way beyond the 'Ask not for whom the bell tolls' recognition of common humanity. The parts should have equal concern for each other. 'If one part suffers, every part suffers with it'.[1] Paul saw his own missionary sufferings, as being for Christ, but also on behalf of the church.[2]

(3) *The family*. Christians are not simply to treat one another as though we were brothers (the church relationship being a watered-down reflection of genetic or blood brotherhood), but because we really are brothers and sisters in Christ, all alike equally members of the household of God. And this is true at both ends of the world: our brother and sister whom we have sent abroad have been able to link up with other brothers and sisters in Christ, whom we have

never met. Years ago I was rummaging through files of Japanese student literature way back in the early fifties: and I discovered that Japanese Christian students had been praying for British Christian students engaged in a Mission to the University in Cambridge. They were praying for me and my friends while we were in university, and we were not praying for them, or even consciously aware of their existence. They were theologically and biblically way ahead of where we had been at that time.

Sending a missionary to any particular country brings us in touch with other members of God's worldwide family and enables us all to become aware that relationship to some extent. One of our friends in Hakodate, not yet a brother as he became, was unemployed and suffering from lung tuberculosis: we mentioned him and asked for prayer in a letter. Out of the blue came a gift for this needy friend from Sir John Laing, head of Laing Construction in Britain. In Christ, human relationships were being cemented. Communication between senders and sent not only links us together: it establishes fresh links with fellow believers whom we have not known, and makes family a tangible experience.

> Jesus taught us how to live in harmony,
> Jesus taught us how to live in harmony,
> Different faces, different races, he made us one,
> Jesus taught us how to live in harmony.
> Jesus taught us how to be a family,
> Jesus taught us how to be a family,
> Loving one another with the love that he gives,
> Jesus taught us how to be a family.[3]

(4) *The army.* As we have seen in the chapter on Prayer, we belong to the Lord's army locked in battle with the spiritual forces of wickedness: and while the illustration of our

corporate armour is outlined in Ephesians 6:10–17, it is the following verses 18–20 which describe the method of fighting, namely by prayer. We cannot make a cowardly withdrawal and leave those we have sent pinned down in no-man's land or imprisoned in the enemies' hands. We have to be as much committed to the battle as they are. As we pray in our homes or in small gatherings within our local church structure, or as a whole congregation, we are engaged in the same spiritual battle as they are.

2. Why Missionaries Need to Keep in Touch with their Senders

(1) Those of us who are missionaries are under obligation to them. We were sent out by them; they are supporting us and praying for us. That is not easy for them in their busy lives serving Christ in the home country; it requires determination, persistence and imagination. But their imagination has limits, unless we feed them with realistic information, so that they can pray for us intelligently. It is difficult to pray with no fresh information for weeks and months. We have to recognise that our work is their work too, and it is our responsibility to allow them to participate, to enable them to take ownership, to feel that they are working here in our overseas situation through their prayers, joining in our struggle.

(2) We are united by our praying. They may be a week away by letter, a day away by plane. The time difference may be a few hours. But because of the omnipresence of God, when they pray and we pray, it becomes simultaneous. The action may be over here on the other side of the world, but prayer brings the praying senders right into the scene of the action. We have to work at it, and they have to work at it, to see that we synchronise in prayer.

(3) Our senders are dependent upon the quality and realism of our communication. Our danger is that writing prayer letters and newsletters can seem like a monthly or quarterly chore. The pile of unanswered letters seems daunting in view of all the other calls upon our time. Just living can take up an awful lot of time in some environments, especially if we have a family to take care of. But we need to see communicating as part of our total picture: with a deep sense of gratitude that other people want to be involved by praying for us. They need to know what to pray for. Sometimes home churches do become dilatory or disinterested, but those abroad are at least partially responsible for this, because we have either not written (or sent cassettes) at all, or even if we have, not effectively communicated our needs for prayer, or been sufficiently frank about our real feelings. J O Fraser opened his heart to those who were praying for him. It's well worth reading *Mountain Rain*, by his daughter Eileen Crossman, to see that.

3. Conclusion – Six Truths

The New Testament sees the task of making disciples of all nations and planting a Christian church in every community as the responsibility of the whole church, to take the whole gospel to the whole world. This remains true today:

TRUE: It is not just a task for the 1% of church members who are sent, but also for the 99% who send them. To be a sender is just as much part of obedient Christian discipleship, as being a goer. And there is no hierarchy of vocations; overseas missionaries, homeside professional ministers and 'lay people' do not vary in their degree of commitment to Christ's cause – at least, not in terms of the job they do!

TRUE: With the increasing mix of races, 'the mission field' has come to us. Not all churches have yet discovered how to be effective in cross cultural evangelism, and the pressures of a tolerant pluralistic society make it no easier.

TRUE: In our towns and cities, we should be praying for national churches and emerging groups of national believers overseas, but our own chosen and sent representatives provide a wonderful link and channel of communication between us.

TRUE: ALL of us have a responsibility to go out into the society in which we live and work and witness for Christ. But more than ever before, we live in a global village, and those we send provide a natural bridge across language barriers with people who live at a distance removed from us.

TRUE: Today more countries stand open to evangelism and church planting than at any time since the outbreak of the 1914–18 War. And there are more people living in those countries than ever before.

But it is **SUPREMELY TRUE** that the unfinished task in countries where the Christian church is either virtually non-existent, or a tiny oppressed minority, still calls churches to send some of their most gifted members. That 'sending' is a much more significant role than many of us have realised up till this time. That is the key message of this book.

Notes

1 1 Corinthians 12:25,26
2 Colossians 1:24
3 Graham Kendrick, 1986 (Eastbourne: Thankyou Music)

BIBLIOGRAPHY

Books

Balfour, Graham. *Life of Robert Louis Stevenson*

Birks, Herbert. *Life and Correspondence of Thomas Valpy French, First Bishop of Lahore*. London: John Murray, 1895

Borthwick, Paul. *A Mind for Missions*. Colorado: Navpress, 1987

Borthwick, Paul. *Youth and Missions*. Wheaton, Ill.: Scripture Press, 1988

Borthwick, Paul. *How to be a World Class Christian*. Wheaton, Ill.: Scripture Press, 1991

Church Missions Policy Handbook. Wheaton, Ill.: Association of Church Missions Committees, 1987

Crossman, Eileen. *Mountain Rain: A new biography of James O. Fraser*, Sevenoaks: OMF Books, 1982

Fraser, Mrs. J. O. *Fraser and Prayer*. London: China Inland Mission, 1963

Goldsmith, Martin. (Ed.) *Love your Local Missionary*. London: MARC Europe, STL, Evangelical Missionary Alliance, 1984.

Griffiths, Michael C. *Get your Church Involved in Missions!* London: OMF Books, 1972

Griffiths, Michael (Ed.). *Ten Sending Churches*. London: MARC Europe; STL; Evangelical Missionary Alliance, 1985

Hock, Roland F. *The Social Context of Paul's Ministry: Tentmaking and Apostleship*. Philadelphia: Fortress Press, 1980

Hopkins, Hugh Evan. *Charles Simeon of Cambridge*. London: Hodder & Stoughton, 1977

Jeremias, Joachim. *Jerusalem in the Time of Jesus*. London: SCM Press, 1969

Johnstone, Patrick. *Operation World*. Carlisle: O M Publishing, 1993

Jordan, Peter. *Re-entry: Making the Transition from Missions to Life at Home*. Seattle: YWAM Publishing, 1992

Kraemer, Hendrik. *The Christian Message in a Non-Christian World*. London: Edinburgh House Press, 1938

Lovett, Richard. *James Chalmers his autobiography and letters*. London: RTS, 1903

Mackay, J. W. *Mackay of Uganda*. London: Hodder & Stoughton, 1898

Morgan, Jill. *A Man of the Word: Life of G. Campbell Morgan*. London: Pickering and Inglis, 1951

O'Connor, Jerome Murphy. *St.Paul's Corinth: Texts and Archeology*. Minnesota: Liturgical Press, 1983

Paton, James (Ed.) *The Story of Dr.John G.Paton's Thirty Years with South Sea Cannibals*. New York: George Doran Co.

Piggin, Stuart & Roxburgh, John. *The St.Andrew's Seven*. Edinburgh: Banner of Truth, 1885

Pirolo, Neal. *Serving as Senders*. O.M. Publishing, 1996

Taylor, Mrs. Howard. *Behind the Ranges: Fraser of Lisuland*

S.W. *China*. London: Lutterworth Press & C.I.M., 1944

Thiessen, Gerd. *Social Setting of Pauline Christianity*. Philadelphia: Fortress Press, 1982 and T & T Clark, Edinburgh

Torjeson, Edvard. *The Missiological Ministry of Fredrik Franson*. Monograph, 1985

A Study of Fredrik Fransen: The development of his Ecclesiology, Missiology and Worldwide Evangelism. Ann Arbor: University Microfilms International, 1985

Tucker, Ruth. *From Jerusalem to Irian Jaya*. Grand Rapids: Zondervan, 1983

Ward, Ted. *Living Overseas: A book of preparations*. London: Collier Macmillan, 1984

Warneck, Gustav. *Missionsstunden*. Gutersloh, 1878–1897

Wilson, J. Christy. *Today's Tentmakers*. Wheaton: Tyndale House Publishers, 1979

Yamamori, T. *God's New Envoys*. Portland: Multnomah Press, 1987

Journal and Magazine Articles

Broomhall, Benjamin. *China's Millions*, 1894

Griffiths, Valerie. 'The Teachers of Righteousness.' *The Westminster Record*, 1995

Hock, Roland F. 'The Workshop as a Social Setting for Paul's Missionary Preaching.' *Catholic Biblical Quarterly* 1979, Vol.41. No.3

Kasdorf, Hans. *Article in Missiology*, July 1980

Pattisson, Peter. 'The Trouble with Tentmakers', *East Asia's Millions*

Torjeson, Edvard. 'The Legacy of Fredrik Franson'. *International Bulletin of Missionary Research*, July 1991

APPENDIX

The following statement is used by a wide range of churches from various denominations. If you would like to amend it for your church, you are welcome to do so. It is available on disk from the Chairman of the Mission Council, Gold Hill Baptist Church, Chalfont St Peter, Bucks SL9 9DG, United Kingdom. Tel: (0)1753 887173 Fax: (0)1753 892572. (For overseas callers add the prefix of the calling country plus 44)

Gold Hill Overseas Policy Statement

1. Introduction

1.1 A Definition of Mission: Its Biblical Basis

The Body of Christ at Gold Hill seeks to appropriate the authority of the Lord Jesus and to fulfil the great commission which He gave to His Church: 'Go therefore and make disciples of all nations, baptising them in the name of the Father and of the Son and of the Holy Spirit, teaching them to observe all that I have commanded you'. (Matthew

28:19–20; cf. Mark 16:15–18; Luke 24:46–49; Acts 1:7–8)

Though caring ministries would also play an important role in this strategy, we emphasise direct evangelism and ministries and gifts which, when exercised in the power of the Holy Spirit, facilitate evangelisation, church planting, teaching and discipling.

1.2 Extent of responsibility

God's people are commanded by the Lord Jesus to be witnesses 'in Jerusalem and in all Judea and Samaria and to the ends of the earth'. To facilitate the effective administration of the Fellowship's fulfilment of its commission, the following areas of responsibility are recognised:

1.2.1 Jerusalem – Local evangelism and church growth resides within the responsibility of the church leadership.

1.2.2 Judea – Gold Hill UK (GH UK) is responsible for the extension ministry of the fellowship within the United Kingdom in accordance with GH UK policy document.

1.2.3 The ends of the earth – Gold Hill Overseas (GO) is responsible for overseas mission, particularly those members working overseas and at the home bases of mission organisations. Gold Hill Overseas will co-operate with other departments of the church in matters of cross-cultural mission in the UK.

1.3 Intention

This policy statement is designed to ensure that the great commission is carried out by establishing a clear sense of direction, maintaining momentum and acting as a framework within which decisions can be made. It is intended to be flexible and adaptable so that changes can be effected as the committee would agree under the guidance and the control of the Holy Spirit. The document will therefore be reviewed every five years and revised as necessary.

2 Composition of Board

2.1 Membership
The Board comprises approximately between 10 and 12 members, according to need, and includes the following:

- Chairman
- Vice Chairman
- Secretary (ex officio deacon)
- Treasurer (ex officio deacon)

The Board will be organised into three sub-committees with responsibilities as listed in section 3.

2.2 Appointment and Term of Office
Appointment of members is made by a recommendation of the Board to the Eldership, subject to ratification annually by the Church Meeting, from among Church members with a proven interest and involvement in the missionary life of the Church. The term of office is indefinite but should be reviewed every three years.

2.3 Responsibilities of Board Members
- To attend Board Meetings (usually monthly).
- To maintain viable links with the missionaries and the candidates assigned to them.
- To be familiar with Board policy.
- To spend between 5 and 10 hours a month on mission business.

- To attend Board occasional days in order to consider mission strategy.
- To pray for missionary work.

3 Responsibilities of officers and committees

The Board's responsibility is to act as the Church's executive arm with regard to mission, giving advice on all aspects of missionary activity and formulating specific proposals for the consideration and approval of the Eldership and the Church Meeting, particularly those involving an extension of our missionary outreach.

3.1 Mission Board Officers

3.1.1 Chairman

- To undertake overall leadership of the Board
- To chair Board meetings
- To take chairman's action, whenever necessary, seeking advice if appropriate
- To act as a link with the eldership and church meeting
- To make recommendations for new members of the Board as required
- To seek guidance for the future direction of church missionary policy, initiating a regular review and appraisal of the policy document.

3.1.2 Secretary

- To undertake the non-financial administration duties of the Board
- To keep minutes of Board meetings
- To distribute mail and information to the committees of the Board

- To ensure that appropriate records are kept by committees of the Board
- To serve on the Administrative Committee

3.1.3 Treasurer

- To control the financial activities of the Board
- To prepare an annual missionary budget
- To distribute missionary allowances, candidates' financial support and other gifts
- To arrange pension provision for our missionaries where appropriate
- To handle all correspondence relating to finance
- To act as a link with the Finance Board, the Church Trust and the Diaconate
- To serve on the Administrative Committee.

3.2 *Administrative Sub-Committee*

3.2.1 To assist the Treasurer in the management of the Board's finances

3.2.2 To publicise the church's missionary work:

- by publishing *GO* magazine
- by producing literature and resource materials
- by providing a news board in the church building
- by selecting delegates to represent the Board with other churches, societies or agencies if required
- to arrange Sunday evening missionary services, away days and other occasional meetings.

3.3 *Members' Sub-Committee*

3.3.1 To maintain accurate lists of sponsored members and Associate Members

3.3.2 To make preparation for members going out to the field for the first time

- by arranging and publicising valedictories and farewell meetings
- by ascertaining the missionary's needs from the Society, and establishing appropriate support levels in association with the Treasurer
- by appointing a committee member to act as the Board's link with the missionary
- by ensuring that a prayer team is set up by the missionary's House Fellowship
- by informing the missionary of the need to provide regular information and photographs for the GO newsheet and to the prayer team.

3.3.3 To maintain contact with the missionary in the field

- by corresponding regularly (at least bi-monthly)
- by relaying news to GO newsheet, the church bulletin, the prayer team and the church meeting
- by offering counsel and advice where necessary
- by assisting the Treasurer in re-evaluation of support levels each year
- by making recommendations concerning pastoral visits or short mid-term holidays in the UK

3.3.4 To make preparation for the missionary's furlough

- by helping the missionary, in conjunction with the society, to establish the programme for the furlough (holiday, training, deputation, etc.)
- by reserving the mission house or other accommodation

- by arranging, in conjunction with the prayer team and house fellowships, that the missionary is met at the airport and that a welcome home is organised
- by publicising the missionary's return by the normal channels.

3.3.5 To facilitate the smooth running of the missionary's furlough

- by ensuring that provision made for the missionary's accommodation, finance and pastoral care is adequate
- by encouraging the missionary's contacts with house fellowships, youth groups, and other appropriate church organisations
- by ensuring that reports are made to the church meeting and the Members' Committee
- by monitoring the missionary's spiritual progress, arranging counselling and ministry if necessary
- by organising the missionary's return to the field

3.3.6 To maintain various home-end missionary activities of the church

- by undertaking the running of the Mission House, including bookings and finance.
- by contact with other missionary minded churches and the Evangelical Missionary Alliance.

3.3.7 To supervise the organisation of missionary prayer teams

- by maintaining lists of teams and their leaders
- by encouraging the prayer life of the teams, particularly by attendance at their meetings

3.3.8 To have special responsibilities towards those missionaries sent out directly from the Church who are not with a missionary organisation, (Section 6).

3.4 *Candidates' Sub-Committee*

The Candidates' Sub-Committee is a joint committee working with Gold Hill UK with special responsibilities for providing counsel and guidance to those candidates training for overseas mission and pastoral ministry within the UK.

3.4.1 To maintain accurate lists of candidates at Bible School or Missionary College, on short-term service and in training at Gold Hill.

3.4.2 To welcome and encourage all those expressing an interest in full-time service at home or overseas, offering practical guidance and spiritual counsel where appropriate.

3.4.3 To recognise and authenticate the candidate's firm call to serve the Lord.

3.4.4 To seek the Lord's will with the candidate as to training and preparation, including ministry within the church, short-term service at home or overseas and choice of college and course.

3.4.5 To recommend to the Board any needs for short-term financial support during the training period.

3.4.6 To seek, with the candidate, the choice of an appropriate society or agency with which the call may be fulfilled, attending interviews with the candidate if necessary.

3.4.7 To monitor the candidate's spiritual progress, arranging for ministry or counsel as necessary, and conducting a formal interview at the appropriate time.

3.4.8 To make a final recommendation of acceptance, ensuring that it is approved by the Mission Board, the eldership and the church meeting.

3.4.9 To transfer the candidate and his records to the Members' Committee at the end of the period of training and preparation.

4 The preparation of missionaries

The Board's prime responsibility in fulfilling the Great Commission is prayerfully to identify those who have the call of God upon them and present them with the challenge of this call upon their lives, preferably before they have become well settled in a secular career or in marriage. They will then require training, within and outside the Church, careful counselling and pastoring and placement in a suitable work, usually with a missionary society. The Fellowship is looking for its most gifted members for the Lord's work of mission.

4.1 Recruitment and Selection Procedures

The following procedures will normally be followed:

4.1.1 Candidates should have been in membership for a sufficiently long time to ensure that their spiritual integrity is unquestioned. They should be aware of the importance of body life through attendance at their House Fellowship.

4.1.2 They will normally seek the recommendation of their Elder, House Fellowship Leader or Youth Leader. There will be a recognition of their spiritual gifts and clear evidence of the Lord's blessing upon their service in the church in addition to any personal desire they may have to serve the Lord. They should normally have reached the age of eighteen years before going through the formal procedures.

4.1.3 Candidates will be interviewed by members of the Candidates' Sub-Committee and will be counselled and pastored by the member or members to whom supervision of their progress is entrusted (3.4).

4.1.4 Candidates should be in agreement with the doctrinal basis of the Church and with our understanding of the full gospel of Christ.

4.1.5 After recommendation from the Board, a candidate's call will be confirmed by the Eldership and the Church meeting.

4.1.6 Where any applicant's approach to the Board is considered, after interview, to be premature for reason of age, lack of spiritual maturity or for any other reason, he or she will be encouraged to take up some form of active service in the Church and to become committed to his or her House Fellowship. The application to the Board will be reported to the candidate's Elder and House Fellowship leader who will pay particular attention to his or her spiritual progress.

4.2 Training

The Church expects our missionaries to move under the direction of the Holy Spirit, to grow steadily in spiritual maturity, to be equipped to handle spiritual warfare and to be effective in service. Therefore, before a candidate's call can finally be confirmed, he or she must submit to some or all of the following forms of practical and formal training:

- Service in some area of the Gold Hill Fellowship.
- Experience in some evangelistic work in another area of the United Kingdom.
- Short term service overseas.
- Formal training in a recognised Bible College or Missionary Training College.
- Participation in the Christian Service Training programme of the church.

4.3 Members working abroad

Where members or associates wish to serve abroad for shorter or longer periods, either in their normal professional capacity, or in VSO-type schemes, they may apply to the Candidates' Sub-Committee for advice and counselling. Responsibility for their pastoral care and prayer support would remain with their House Fellowship elder and leaders. The Members' Sub-Committee will give any specialist help where necessary.

4.4 Associate Members

Associate Membership is a special category of Church membership for those persons who already are members of another church either in another part of the UK or overseas. Because of Gold Hill's proximity to both the British Headquarters of WEC International and Wycliffe Bible Translators many of their home-base staff attend the Church regularly. Associate Membership is therefore a means by which they may participate actively within the life of the church whilst recognising their commitment to their sending church. Associate Membership will only be given in full consultation with the sending church.

5 Missionaries with missionary organisations

The Board recognises its responsibility to advise candidates upon the choice of the society to which they will commit themselves. They will be encouraged to investigate the potentialities of as many societies as are appropriate to their call.

5.1 Suitability of mission organisation

Criteria for the evaluation of a society would include the following:

5.1.1 It should have a general doctrinal agreement and unity in the Spirit with the Church at Gold Hill.

5.1.2 It needs to be properly directed, organised, administered and financed.

5.1.3 Its goals and objectives should be clearly articulated and be approved by the Church. It must be of sufficient size to ensure that its goals and objectives can be effectively realised.

5.1.4 Its missionary methods should be appropriate to its fields of activity and to its size.

5.1.5 The general welfare of the missionary should be seen to be a matter of partnership with the Church.

5.1.6 It should have a sympathetic attitude to the missionary's family responsibilities.

5.1.7 The Board will not confine our involvement entirely to societies with which we already have close relations. We will always be guided by the witness of the Spirit.

Candidates will be carefully counselled to ensure that they commit themselves to effectual and suitable societies.

5.2 *Commitment to the mission organisation*

Gold Hill Overseas recognises the important role played by missionary organisations in overseas mission and duly commits its members into the care and direction of the organisation.

5.2.1　Once candidates have been accepted by a society they will be accountable to the established leadership of the society.

5.2.2　They are to follow the principles and practices of the mission. GO will seek to co-operate with the particular mission organisation to ensure that the missionary's ministry is effective and fruitful. Reference to pastoral care of missionaries, Section 8.

6　Gold Hill Missionaries

Although the general policy of Gold Hill Overseas is that missionaries are sent out through established missionary organisations, there may be occasions when missionaries go direct from the fellowship to their field of service. This option will only occur if:

a) There is no suitable missionary organisation working in the area.
b) There are special local situations making this option the most appropriate.

6.1 *Overseas Assignment*

6.1.1　Placement of missionaries will only be done in close

fellowship with the GO Mission Board. This may require a visit to the area by an appropriate member of the Board prior to the deployment of the missionary.

6.1.2 A job-description of the nature of the missionary's assignment will be drafted to provide guidelines to all concerned.

6.2 Local Fellowship and Pastoral Care

There must be those within the field with whom the missionary can have fellowship and receive a degree of pastoral care. The Members' Committee will maintain regular contact with those concerned.

6.3 Finance

These missionaries will be classed as SPONSORED MISSIONARIES, and the normal procedure for assessing the level of support will be applied (Section 10.3.1).

6.3.1 GO will pay for Home Assignment fares, but would expect missionaries to budget for their own holidays out of their support funds.

6.3.2 GO will pay for any approved language study.

6.3.3 Local medical insurance will be arranged where possible.

6.3.4 GO will pay Class 3 National Insurance.

6.4 Home Assignment/Furlough

It would be normally expected that a term of overseas assignment would be for three years. During a three-year term, a Home Assignment will be for three months and may include:-

- Rest and Refreshment
- Reunion with family and friends
- Renewal of links with church fellowship
- Attending a training course of some kind (8.5)
- Involvement in the fellowship life of Gold Hill.
- Reporting to and sharing with GO on developments of the missionary work, and prayerful planning for the future.

6.5 Holiday

Holiday periods will normally consist of four weeks each year. In the case of a Home Assignment being due, missionaries may have the option of saving the four weeks' holiday for that year and adding them on to the three months at home, so making four months in all.

6.6 Family Responsibilities

In an emergency the missionary must feel free to make arrangements to come home in a hurry, for example a death or major illness in their immediate family. GO would be sympathetic to helping with costs in such instances. In the case of a family event, such as a wedding, this would be seen as a family responsibility, if it did not come within the Home Assignment period.

6.7 Decisions

Day to day decisions are to be taken by missionaries, but any major decisions relating to future ministry, training, etc. should be referred to the Mission Board. The Members' Committee will take special responsibility for the pastoral care of GO missionaries.

7 The Development of Prayer Support

This is the most important aspect of missionary support and requires the energetic commitment of the whole Board and the Church. It will, however, be the special responsibility of the members committee.

7.1 Prayer needs will be publicised in the Bulletin and GO news, by prayer times in Sunday services, especially mission services and communions, and during Church meetings.

7.2 Church members will be encouraged to pray regularly and consistently for at least one missionary, either privately or as a member of a prayer team, or both.

7.3 Prayer Teams will provide for in-depth intercession in the power of the Holy Spirit for individual missionaries.

7.4 House Fellowships will develop prayer for their missionary normally by supplying the team leader and by encouraging their members to attend the team, as well as by prayer during normal Fellowship meetings.

7.5 Each missionary should be encouraged to ensure that there is an adequate communication of prayer needs by letter or by tape.

8 Pastoral Care of Missionaries

Though missionaries with missionary organisations will always be in submission to their Mission leaders. GO missionaries, on the other hand, will relate to the Member's Committee and through them to the whole Mission Board

(Section 6.8). GO will continue to offer pastoral care in consultation with the society and in the following ways:

8.1 Every missionary will be firmly linked with a House Fellowship and will receive comfort and succour of both a practical and spiritual nature from their group. This will supplement the main prayer support offered by their Prayer Team and will ensure that they continue to experience life in the Body of Christ.

8.2 The Board recognises the importance of pastoral visits for serving missionaries. Such visits will be organised according to the availability of finance and pastoral staff, and may also be made by members visiting the missionaries' fields of service.

8.3 The Church will endeavour to provide, and the Board or its representative will administer, a Mission House in the immediate locality of Gold Hill. It will serve as a home and base for the spiritual and physical refreshment of our own missionaries and of missionaries and Christian workers from outside our Fellowship. No missionary should be unable to use the house through lack of finance, though the house should be largely self-financing.

8.4 The society will be encouraged to allow the missionary on furlough to spend as much time as possible at Gold Hill, so that relationships may be renewed and support built up, the Church instructed and informed about the work in the field, and the missionary refreshed physically, mentally and spiritually.

8.5 Missionaries will be encouraged to undertake periods of in-service training and refresher courses either in the field or during furlough. Books and cassette recordings of Church services and teaching sessions will also be regularly distributed through the House Fellowships.

8.6 The Board will maintain close links with the sponsoring society, thus ensuring that we receive regular reports upon the missionary's progress and situation for which it is totally responsible through the field director. However, the Board may, on occasions, initiate dialogues with the society, where pastoral concern indicates that our missionary is unable to function under scriptural principles in the situation or circumstances to which he or she is posted.

8.7 Our responsibility for the reasonable educational, welfare and pastoral needs of our missionary families is also recognised by the Board.

8.8 Pastoral care for missionaries will not cease with retirement. They will be encouraged to resettle near Gold Hill where they can remain under the care of the fellowship and where accomodation may be able to be made available.

8.9 If a missionary's husband or wife is not a member of Gold Hill, the partner has the option of becoming an 'Associate Member' whilst still retaining full membership with his or her sending church. GO will seek to co-operate with the sending church of the other partner in matters of pastoral care and Home Assignment.

9 The Education of the Church in Mission

Teaching on mission should be an integral part of the Church's educational programme. It may be encouraged by the following means:

9.1 Educational programmes will be organised to instruct and inspire the Church through the House Fellowships, youth organisations, the Bible School, and the Christian Service Training programme.

9.2 Regular reports will be presented to Church meetings, particularly as a stimulus for prayer.

9.3 Mission will feature regularly in Sunday services, normally in the evening, but, where appropriate, and as guided by the Spirit, in the morning teaching programme.

9.4 All available forms of educational technology will be used to communicate information about mission and about our missionaries. Use will be made of programmes and materials produced by missionary agencies and societies.

9.5 Experienced missionaries and missionary 'statesmen' will be invited, from time to time, to speak to the Church. Missionary conferences may be organised.

9.6 Members, particularly young people, will be encouraged to attend missionary conferences (10.6.3).

10 Missionary Finance

10.1 *The Missionary Budget*

The budget is the mechanism used by the Mission and the Finance Boards to ensure that, as far as possible, all Gold Hill missionaries are supported according to their needs. The Mission Budget is set as a percentage of the total Church budget and is normally not less than 33% of that total. It is the intention of the church that funding of GO and GH UK should increase to 50% of the total Church budget.

The GO budget is to be authorised by the Church Meeting after consideration and adoption by the Mission Board, the Finance Board, the Diaconate and the Eldership.

10.2 Budget Distribution

Budget headings cover all areas of our missionary activity, *ie*:

- Missionary preparation and training
- Missionary support
- Missionary pastoral care, including pastoral visits, etc.
- Missionary education and in-service training
- Church education in mission
- Contingency

The main emphasis of funding policy lies in the direction of the preparation and training of new missionaries and the continuing support of missionaries already in service. No specific support level is guaranteed, but the Church sees the provision of funds adequate to the needs of the mission-ary as its responsibility before the Lord and as one of the most important faith dimensions of life in the Body of Christ.

We give priority to the support of missionaries who are in membership at Gold Hill rather than to societies, agencies or specific projects, whether denominational or inter-denomi-national. Furthermore, stress is laid upon the support of evangelistic outreach rather than programmes involving social action alone. Within these parameters funding is established according to the following categories:

10.2.1 'SPONSORED' MISSIONARIES: These are those who have grown up spiritually within the church, whose call

was received while they were active in the church, and whose call was authenticated by the church leadership. It also includes those who have established long-term relationships with the Church, and have been adopted as sponsored missionaries.

10.2.2 'ASSOCIATE' MISSIONARIES: Those who joined the Church after their missionary commitment had begun. In such cases, the missionaries may already have a sending Church, and are therefore accepted as 'Associate Members' of Gold Hill Baptist Church in agreement with the sending church. Support for such missionaries may develop as they become more known to the Fellowship and may well be organised initially through their House Fellowship.

10.2.3 MISSION OR DEVELOPMENT AGENCIES: Support for mission and development ministries such as TEAR Fund, UBS and FEBA, may be given on special occasions, even where we have no personnel actively in service with them.

10.2.4 Support for other missionaries, societies and agencies which have no direct connection with the Church may result from giving specifically designated by individual Church members, but not through our Mission Budget. Church members who proceed to missionary service without the agreement and recommendation of the Board and the Eldership may expect no support other than personal gifts of this kind. In the case of extreme hardship, grants may be made as an expression of our love and concern.

10.3 Level of Support

Support will provide a standard of living related to that of the local population where the missionary is serving, as determined by the relevant society or agency. Allocations are adjusted annually in line with increases in the cost of living and inflation as recommended by the society and also in accordance with changes in family circumstances.

10.3.1 SPONSORED MISSIONARIES: It is recognised that missionaries may have financial support from other churches or friends. The Gold Hill support system is designed to act as a "top-up" system, making up the difference between a missionary's existing support, and his/her full support. The required level of support will be ascertained by means of an annual financial report provided by the missionary at the request of the Treasurer. This will present the total anticipated needs for the next twelve months, and the income from all sources outside of Gold Hill. In the light of these estimates GO will set a budgeted amount for the missionary making up the support level to 100%.

10.3.2 ASSOCIATE MISSIONARIES: Associate missionaries may expect little or no direct financial support. However, after a suitable period of membership, which will be no less than two years and/or one furlough spend largely in the Fellowship, they may graduate to the 'sponsored' category.

10.4 Duration of Support

Full missionary support will normally begin with departure to the field and continue throughout service, as long as there is need. Special requirements for equipment may be met by love gifts from the missionary's House Fellowship or, if necessary, by grants from the Board.

Support may be withdrawn for any of the following reasons:

- The missionary is no longer in membership at Gold Hill and has alternative sources of support.
- He or she is no longer in agreement with the doctrinal basis of the church.
- He or she is no longer in submission to the Leadership of the church.
- He or she has returned home and is well able to accept responsibility for his or her own support.

Field leaders will be requested to make brief annual reports on the missionary's service. There will thus be a continuing process of evaluation of the missionary's progress.

10.5 *Insurance and Retirement Policy*

Where a missionary's society recommends payment of National Insurance contributions and/or retirement fund payments this is effected by the Board through normal support channels.

Where there is no retirement provision or where pension payments are voluntary, it is the intention of GO to make provision for an index-linked Gold-Hill pension scheme through private insurance which will ensure that all missionaries can expect similar provision upon retirement. In the case of premature termination of service, missionaries should then be able to take over the payment of premiums.

Older missionaries for whom there is no such provision will require continued support in retirement to ensure an adequate standard of living.

10.6 *Support for Candidates in Training*

10.6.1 Short Term Workers.

An important feature of the training programme is to give candidates experience of living by faith. They should, therefore, seek their own support for short-term projects. However, if they have already funded their experience in the United Kingdom themselves, the Board will consider making a substantial grant as a contribution to their travel and living expenses for short-term work abroad depending upon costs. Each cases will be considered upon its merits.

10.6.2 Bible and Missionary College Students –
Where the Lord's call is upon a candidate's life and he or she has completed the Board's selection and training programme and is unable to obtain LEA or other grants, the Board will make interest free loans to cover fees and living costs. This loan will be up to a maximum of 100% of the fees and maintenance whilst at college. Candidates are normally expected to make a contribution form their own funds for their training.

Repayment of these loans will be waived in the event of the candidate's completing four years of missionary service. Any special difficulty of repayment would be treated sympathetically.

10.6.3 National or International Conferences –
Some help may be offered to young people, when suitably recommended, so that they may attend such conferences. Criteria for grant aid would include their potential for missionary service as well as financial need.

10.7 *Contingency Fund*

The Contingency Fund serves is a source of funding for unforeseen emergencies. All other financial needs are met under the appropriate headings.

10.8 *Allocation of Surpluses*

At the end of the financial year, any surpluses in the Mission account may, according to need and as the Board determines, be distributed in any of the following ways:

- Allocation to approved mission agencies
- Appropriation for the same or other headings in the following year's budget.
- Allocation to special projects, normally associated with one of our own missionaries.

10.9 *Legacies and Special Gifts*

Legacies and gifts are distributed according to the wishes of the legator or donor. Where there is no designation, the Board will make an allocation by the normal fund mechanism, reserving the right to carry over money into subsequent financial years or to allocate it, with Eldership approval, to some special unbudgeted project.

10.10 *Funding of Deficits*

When the mission budget is in deficit at the end of the financial year or projections show the likelihood of such, the shortage may be offset in one of the following ways:

- An appeal be made to church members to increase their giving as a token of their responsibility before the Lord to provide for those he has called.
- Transference of funds from the Church General Fund to the mission fund.
- A special gift and self-denial day, with prayer and fasting, be called.
- A reduction be made in giving to approved agencies.
- In extremis, an across-the-board percentage reduction be made in missionary allowance.

11 Conclusion

The members of Gold Hill Baptist Church hereby seek to fulfil their responsibilities as regards to the Great Commission. In so doing we aim to see the Kingdom of God extended, and the Name of Jesus glorified throughout the earth. Maranatha! Come Lord Jesus!

Two Leaflets from OMF to help you pray

How to pray for Missionaries and *How to Pray for Professionals Overseas* are available from OMF International, Station Approach, Borough Green, SEVENOAKS, Kent, TN15 8BG. Tel: 01732 887299. These leaflets give practical help on how to pray for people, whatever country they are working in. Please state the number of copies you would like. There is no charge.

English Speaking OMF Centres

OMF International
Station Approach
Borough Green
Sevenoaks
Kent
TN15 8BG

OMF
PO Box 849
Epping
NSW 2121
AUSTRALIA

OMF
PO Box 10–159
Balmoral
Auckland 1
NEW ZEALAND

OMF
5759 Coopers Avenue
Mississauga ON
L4Z 1R9
CANADA

OMF
10 West Dry Creek Circle
Littleton
CO 80120–4413
USA

OMF
2 Cluny Road
Singapore 1025
REPUBLIC OF SINGAPORE

OMF
PO Box 5341
Kenilworth 7745
SOUTH AFRICA

OMF is on the world wide web at http://www.omf.org

Bosshardt: a Biography

by Jean Watson

Alfred Bosshardt is one of the most remarkable missionaries of the twentieth century. He played a key role in the development of modern China.

Born in Manchester in 1897, Alfred was accepted for training by the OMF (then the China Inland Mission) in 1920. Within two years he departed for the huge and dangerous land of China.

At that period China was highly unstable. Local warlords controlled many areas, and the Communists and Nationalists struggled for power. All missionaries were seen as spies, and in 1934 Communist guerrillas captured Alfred and his wife Rose. Rose was released, but Alfred was forced to join the Red Army on the weary trek which became known as the Long March. He trudged 2,500 miles.

Alfred's knowledge of both Chinese and French was invaluable, since the only accurate map of the region was in French. The way he shared his knowledge, and maintained a Christlike forbearance despite frequent beatings and threats of execution, has made him a notable figure in modern Chinese history.

'I have learned a lot from his unique experience.'

– JUNG CHANG
Author of *Wild Swans*

 Monarch

ISBN 1 85424 297 0

Hudson Taylor:
Lessons In Discipleship

by Roger Steer

Hudson Taylor (1832–1905) founded the *China Inland Mission* in 1865. Now as *OMF International*, it has around a thousand workers spread across East Asia.

Although he was unremarkable in appearance, Taylor's quiet yet passionate manner inspired hundreds of men and women to go to China as missionaries and many others to pray for its 'lost millions'. In 1900 both the US President and the Mayor of New York came to hear him speak in the Carnegie Hall.

Roger Steer has drawn 100 lessons from Taylor's life and writings on themes such as holiness, prayer, knowing God and the way of the cross. Steer observes, 'Hudson Taylor grew into one of the profoundest Christian thinkers of all time, and his thought has added weight because it arose out of a life of action, forged on the anvil of suffering.'

'Rarely have the personal implications of following Jesus been made so clear.'

– J. I. PACKER

'Hudson Taylor's influence has been immense, right up to the present day. Here is a book that shows us why. It's riveting and full of hope.'

– NIGEL LEE
UCCF

 Monarch

ISBN 1 85424 322 5